UNDER THE FLIGHT PATH

15,000 kms Overland Across Russia, Mongolia & China

SIMON PRIDMORE

Sandsmedia Publishing
BALI, INDONESIA

Sandsmedia Publishing, Bali, Indonesia 80363

www.simonpridmore.com

Book Layout ©2017 Createspace.com and Sandsmedia

Cover Image by Sofie Hostyn

Under the Flight Path/Simon Pridmore. 1st ed.

ISBN-13: 978-1542666862

ISBN-10: 1542666864

For Sofie,
the best travelling companion I could wish for.

Foreword

There is something magical about a great journey. As Alain De Botton says in The Art of Travel, "Journeys are the midwives of thought." As we move through a fresh new landscape, we also move through undiscovered territories in our own mind.

Under the Flight Path is a special travel memoir in that it is a journey in itself. Warm, candid and funny, you feel as if you too are travelling across Russia, Mongolia and China. There is no doubt that Simon and Sofie are seasoned travelling companions, and it is a pleasure to follow them as they navigate new, enriching and unexpected experiences.

I believe you get three types of travellers. Those who are there for physical experiences such as diving and trekking; those who look for social connection and those who are fascinated by the history and culture of a new place. Under the Flight Path, remarkably, combines all three in a quick, easy to read story. Expect to come across knowledge that cannot be found in any guidebook, and that can only be found by tracing the path yourself. It is the type of book where you will be tempted to take notes as you read.

All in all, Under the Flight Path is a journey you will be happy to take. It is a chance to escape and discover evocative new landscapes in the company of Simon and Sofie, who by the end of the novel will feel like friends. You will feel inspired and educated, and quite possibly, compelled to start planning your own journey yourself.

Amy Heydenrych, Author and Founder of "Story"

Preface

For many years, as a British-born cop in colonial Hong Kong, I travelled back and forth between Europe and South China, flying above huge swathes of Europe and Asia that I could never hope to see, because they were communist states. Not only did the countries not encourage western tourism but the nature of my job also prohibited me from visiting them. If I did, my security clearance would be revoked.

Then my life changed and I left that line of work. More importantly, the world changed. Central and Eastern Europe, Russia, Mongolia and China changed and, in 2009, one generation after the Berlin Wall fell and after the bloody denouement to the student occupation of Tiananmen Square, borders were open and independent travel under the flight path that I had taken so many times was now possible.

My wife Sofie and I were moving from Europe to Bali in Indonesia to start a new life there. We had plenty of time, so we decided to do a big chunk of the journey overland, starting in Sofie's hometown of Ghent, Belgium and travelling by train, bus and car across Russia then down through the heart of Mongolia and China. In every country we passed through, we witnessed people and cultures still coming to terms with enormous changes wreaked by the 20th century, while facing the new challenges of the 21st century. We found huge optimism for the future but also a determination to make sure that memories of the past do not fade and will remain as reminders to generations to come. This is their story, as well as ours.

Simon Pridmore, Bali 2017

Table of Contents

§1

Russia

Moscow

Where we find we might be allergic to Lenin and where we have a run-in with minor Russian officialdom, not for the first time.

To arrive in Moscow on the first day of spring is to see the city emerging from its long winter hibernation. As our train rattles through the unappealing suburbs, the last vestiges of the snows of winter can be seen hiding from the sunshine beneath occasional patches of pine forest.

By the time we leave town again, after three days of blue skies and temperatures in the mid-20s, buds of green have appeared in the parks and the earliest flowers are daring to show their colours to promenading couples in tee shirts and summer dresses.

The girls of Moscow, of course, are well ahead of nature in their preparations. By midday on that first day of spring, they are patrolling the boulevards, squares and avenues in mini-skirts and mini-tops, balancing acrobatically on extravagantly contoured and vertigo-inducing platform high-heels. There is a marked contrast between the efforts the Moscow girls make to look their very best and the complete absence of dress sense and disregard for grooming shown by their male counterparts. This is a country where the beaver tail haircut has never gone out of fashion and where a suit can never be too shiny.

This is also a city where, in places, security personnel, both in and out of uniform, often outnumber ordinary citizens. In particular, there are a huge number of uniforms employed in and around Red Square. We saw the entire square sealed off one evening, not by bollards or fencing but by human walls of green and blue.

It is fascinating to look a little more closely at the lady soldiers and policewomen whose footwear is anything but regulation. If your hidden fantasies include women in uniform and high heels, look no further than the officers moving the queues along outside the Lenin Mausoleum.

We visit one morning and join the queue to enter the resting place of the great man, who is looking pretty good for his age. Awkwardly, just as we passed the coffin in which Vladimir Ilyich is laid out in an unfashionable non-shiny, dark suit, I feel an uncontrollable urge to blow my nose, and do so.

The noise echoes like thunder through the darkened room through which we shuffle silently and I tense, waiting for a whistle or a shout. But none comes, so I relax. Evidently, instead of interpreting the explosive ventilation of my nostrils as a mark of disrespect, the guards must have taken it as a symptom of my having been overcome with emotion at being in The Presence. It probably happens all the time.

Even on a quiet day in the mummy queue, you are still not allowed to take your time as you pass by the other memorials to heroes of the Revolution that line the Kremlin wall behind the mausoleum. We pause for a second or two in front of the bust of first cosmonaut Yuri Gagarin to read the plaque below. There is a sharp blast of a whistle nearby. We ignore it. It can't be directed at us, surely. More blasts follow and we look up to see a uniform advancing on us with intent. We move on dutifully. Brezhnev is the next hero in the line and we decide to test the system. Was it just Gagarin we were not supposed to stop at? The whistling begins again and we conclude we have had enough heroes for now. Later in the day, we get similar treatment inside the Kremlin when we try to cross the road in the wrong place. We speculate that we have been singled out and are being followed, but we are probably flattering ourselves.

In Moscow, even today, with the Soviet Union dead and gone twenty years ago, everything you do still involves passing through several levels of security. Just to reach your room in the hotel, you need to manoeuvre your way past the team of heavies at the entrance. Then there is another guy guarding the lift lobby. The final and most daunting obstacle is the lady at the security booth on your floor, who holds your room key and has final control over all comings and goings.

In the Metro there is an official in a box manning each escalator but the entranceways are unmanned and un-gated, which at first seems surprising. It may appear that you can just walk in without paying but be warned. There is no security officer there because it is unnecessary. Try passing through without first waving a valid card over the chip-reader and iron grills spring out automatically from both sides of the entranceway and smash you in the thighs. You only make this mistake once and the bruises take a while to subside. Notwithstanding this, however, the Metro is still hands down the best way to travel around Moscow and, although prices have gone up by 25% over the last two years, tickets are still very cheap.

When you go down into the Metro, especially as you cross from one line to another, it is incredible how quiet it is. Every day, particularly during rush hour, hordes of Muscovite commuters shuffle along the cavernous marble-lined corridors without speaking. All you can hear is the tramp of thousands of feet. It is eerie. Maintaining silence in public is a habit that Russians acquired during the Soviet times, when a loose remark overheard could land you in jail or on a wagon to Siberia.

At least the Metro is quiet. Above ground, Moscow's street noise is deafening, mainly because of the cars. They speed down the wide four lane shopping boulevards creating a ceaseless background roar. Many of them are black, large and expensive. When stationary, they can be found parked half on the road, half on the pavement, or double parked in the middle of the road. A heavy-set, scar-faced driver is usually smoking and glowering threateningly nearby. Even after the ice is long gone, they still rattle noisily along on their metalled winter tyres. Having only ever visited Moscow before in winter, I am surprised by the racket the city makes without its muffling coat of snow.

My previous visits to Moscow were all related to scuba diving. I was in town either to participate in dive exhibitions or to take a train to go up to the Arctic Circle to test diving equipment under sea ice. On a couple of occasions I had small run-ins with the authorities, which may be why I notice their presence everywhere. We have three weeks in Russia ahead of us, we will be travelling off piste a lot and I admit the things I am most apprehensive of are confrontations with petty officialdom.

My first run-in came a few years ago during a brief visit to show off a new range of hi-tech dive computers at a convention at Moscow's Olimpiskiy stadium, as the name suggests, a relic of the 1980 summer Olympic Games. I shipped stand furniture and show samples overland and had to pay a large fee to bring them into the country even temporarily. The shipment arrived intact apart from a couple of DVDs that I had planned to use at the convention to wow audiences with the features and benefits of our expensive new toys. I had ordered a large flat screen TV and

DVD player for the purpose. However, when the rental guys showed up, I sent them away, explaining that, possibly thanks to a light-fingered Russian Customs official I no longer needed any audio-visual equipment. They were upset at the loss of a little business but understood my situation and did not insist.

The next morning, I was trudging through slush on my way to the stadium, my head bowed against snow flurries and a bitter wind, when I perceived someone crossing the road towards me at speed, seemingly intent on a collision course. I had no time to get out of the way and he cannoned into me, sending me reeling back. As he bounced off me, he thrust a package into my chest. I grabbed it instinctively and turned to challenge him but he had already disappeared into the Moscow murk. When I got to the show, I opened the package and found my missing DVDs. At my stand, the TV and player were already set up and a rental invoice was waiting for me on the desk.

My second brush with authority came when I brought into Russia a dozen pre-production computers designed for extreme scuba diving, with the aim of testing them in temperatures of minus 2C under the ice just south of Murmansk. I was also carrying other computers to exhibit at a show in Moscow the following week. So I had a LOT of product with me.

As I passed through airport Customs on the way in, my bags were singled out for physical inspection and I knew I was in trouble. The Customs agent opened the first suitcase and saw the computers all lined up in their boxes. He started shaking his head and muttered "no, no, no, no, not personal effects." He pulled each box open, removed the computer, threw the box on the floor, punched the computer's buttons for a while, then put it aside and started on the next one.

Soon, my little corner of the Customs hall was covered with debris. This was all done without a word and I began to feel intimidated. Was he going to take all the computers away? Was he going to ask for money? Was he going to put me on the first plane back to London? I started to explain what it was all about but he did not react, until I said the word "scuba", at which point he looked at me, raised his hand, indicating that I should stay put, and walked away.

He returned, accompanied by another officer, who, I was given to understand, was a diver. The new officer picked up a computer and started playing with it. The confusion and discomfort in his expression betrayed the fact that he had never seen anything like it. I guessed that he might have given his non-diving colleagues the impression that he was something of a diving guru – the one-eyed man in the land of the scuba-blind, as it were. So, in a bid to help him save face, I started discussing the computer with him, comparing it to others on the market, dropping names and nodding wisely when he pressed a couple of buttons in sequence.

The two officers had a quick discussion and the first motioned to me to repack my case. This took me a good fifteen minutes and when I had finished, I stood up, looked around and saw that the Customs area was completely empty. We must have been between arriving flights. I was alone.

A door opened, the first officer poked his head out and brusquely gestured that I should get out. At least, that was what I understood, so, hoping I had understood correctly and trying not to look to anxious, I speed-walked my way towards the meeters and greeters area. As the crowd parted to let me through and then closed again behind me, I breathed a sigh of relief, feeling like I had just bungee-jumped into Russia.

As I said, perhaps these experiences are behind my focus on the omnipresence of security personnel in Moscow and my concerns over difficulties we may encounter as we travel independently from one end of this vast country to the other. Fortunately, as we are to discover, once you leave the capital, Russia feels much less oppressive and far more laid-back.

Suzdal

Where we take a bus ride perched on half a buttock and spend the night in a monastery.

Our only stop between Moscow and Siberia will take in the two Golden Ring towns of Suzdal and Vladimir. Our ride is train 62 from Moscow Kurskaya Station to Vladimir, travelling second class. It is a top quality "firmenny" train so there is a packed lunch on each seat.

To get from Vladimir to Suzdal we need to take a bus so we cross the open space in front of the station, climb the stairs to the bus ticket office and push the door open to find a hall packed with people. Tempers are fraying as people try and jump from one ticket window to another or push into queues from the side. We use our basic Russian to decipher the timetable, pick out a bus to Suzdal and ask around to find the right queue. We join it at the back and eventually get to the window after half an hour. No one speaks English. Outside Moscow you can't expect English anywhere, not even in hotels. Our tickets have numbers on them so we should get seats. If the number on your ticket is zero, you stand.

Ten minutes before the scheduled 4.30pm departure we go outside and see that our ride, a small, ancient, rusting metal box resting on four almost tread-less tyres, is already there. A crowd is forming so we join it and board a couple of minutes later. The bus fills up quickly. There is no baggage compartment so we sit with rucksacks on our laps, supporting ourselves on half a buttock each. When it seems that no more people can board and the automatic doors have compressed the last couple of passengers into the bus, the driver cranks up the engine and we set off at a lurch in a cloud of black smoke to the tune of cacophonous gear changes. Every window pane and metal plate rattles as we shudder from pothole to pothole along the main road out of town.

And then, incredibly, we stop to let more people on. Somehow the shaking up we have all received since leaving the station has produced more standing room where there was previously none, a bit like the contents of a cereal box settling during transportation. The new arrivals can't get near the driver to pay him directly, so notes and change are passed along the bus. We are largely hidden behind our packs but, as we are sitting right at the front, we are the closest part of the chain to the driver so we do our bit to help the process along.

On the approach to Suzdal, the bus starts to empty and the atmosphere becomes less close and claustrophobic. Suzdal bus station looks like it has been bombed, frequently and recently. It is an unfortunate first impression of what is supposed to be one of the most beautiful towns in Russia. You can get off the bus here and walk into town, but the place looks so inhospitable that we opt to pay a couple more roubles and stay on the bus.

However, when we arrive in the centre of town, we find that the rest of the place is in not much better shape. It looks like a war zone but, to be fair, this is partly due to the fact that we have come upon the town as the seasons are changing. The blanket of winter snow has only just melted away, exposing six months worth of discarded winter trash, and the land and trees lie largely brown and bare, yet to don the green garb of summer.

We load up the backpacks and follow the instructions we have printed out from the Internet to our first choice hostel, which turns out to be a building site. Evidently the images on the hostel's website were a little premature and the product of some creative photoshopping. A boy fishing in the river tells us there is no other accommodation nearby so we head off to try our second choice. This time the instructions take us to a dilapidated monastery on Ulitsa Lenina (Lenin Street - every Russian town has one) that offers rooms. We take their last one, leave the backpacks in our monastic cell and go out to walk the sites while we still have light. We visit the old Kremlin walls, the blue domed cathedral and look over the walls into the Museum of Wooden Architecture. Dinner is in a little restaurant on the main street. The room smells of petrol but the food is wonderful. As we walk back to the monastery, the sky bears the last traces of what must have been a dramatic Suzdal sunset, promising blue skies in the morning.

And sure enough blue skies are delivered as promised but with a chill in the air. The TV in reception tells us it is snowing over the Urals further east and of course that is where our journey is taking us. It is the first of May, a Friday and the beginning of a long holiday weekend for the Russians. Our hostel in the ruined monastery is fully booked tonight so we need to find an alternative. After trying three other places and finding that they are all full too, we decide to spend the morning in Suzdal sightseeing and go back to Vladimir later in the afternoon. Suzdal comes to life in the sunshine, which glints off the golden roofs of the churches and monasteries and warms the colours of the domes, so we do get to see it in all its glory before we depart.

Vladimir

Where there is no room at the inn and we discover that
Beatlemania is not dead.

The ride back down to Vladimir is in an empty bus, a complete contrast from the day before and strange, given that today Suzdal is full of Russians up from the city for the holiday weekend. The night we arrived it was a ghost town but the bus was full. Mind you, the visitors we saw walking around the town this morning did not seem to be the type to take buses, even when their huge black Landcruisers are in for service.

In Vladimir we encounter the same difficulty finding a room as in Suzdal. Eventually, we decide to recruit a taxi driver and we are soon speeding through the suburbs, going from one place to the next on our list without success. We think about camping but we see nowhere that we feel we could safely put up a tent without being harassed. The residential blocks where the hostels are located look like abandoned, bombed out tenements from the outside, with rusty iron bars showing through the walls where the concrete has fallen away in lumps. However, once you creak open the rusted metal security doors and get past the toxic atmosphere of urine and concrete dust on the stairs, the little hotels inside are well decorated, clean and bright with polished wood and glass panels.

None has room for us and, after trying a dozen, we are contemplating the unappealing option of a night in the train station waiting room. Finally, the taxi driver stops listening to us and takes matters into his own hands. He phones a place he knows, which is across the river and out of town. They have a vacancy and we have a bed for the night.

Vladimir is a bustling little city with a fascinating historical past. The next day, we spend some time in the cathedral and a couple of small museums, take a walk in the park and find an excellent shopping mall which has a Spar supermarket where we can stock up on supplies for the train. There's a food court in the mall with sushi, pizza and Baskin and Robbins ice cream for the homesick, as well as a coffee shop with soft armchairs and thick hot chocolate. Vladimir's fashionable youth hang out in the food court and if you half close your eyes, (and close your ears entirely) you could be in a mall in any small town in America. Watching the young Russians at play, it occurs to us that, if these are the leaders and opinion formers of the future, there is every chance that the Russia of the mid 21st century may be more in tune with the West than ever before.

Vladimir is not all about Russia's future, however. In one of the museums, atop an old city gate, is a diorama of the storming of the city by the Mongols in 1238. There is even an English version of the commentary which the staff are very proud of and switch on especially for us, to the consternation of all the local visitors packing the room. Over the next couple of weeks we are going to get a good idea of the huge distance the Mongols had to cover to get here. Indeed, they went much further into Europe, shattering the stability and confidence of long-established feudal societies with hitherto unparalleled levels of force and violence. Viewed from today's perspective, the huge historical impact that a small, sparsely populated country in East Asia had on a vast area of this enormous continent seems an impossible feat.

Invasion is a topic near to the Russian heart. Cultural memories of invasions by the Mongols, Napoleon and Nazi Germany lie very close to the surface of the national consciousness. The victory over the Germans, the battle over Stalingrad and the defence of Moscow are celebrated with a major holiday on May 9th each year and Russians view themselves largely as victims rather than as aggressors. They do not see their nation historically in the expansionist and colonial light that many non-Russians do.

In Vladimir at one point we go up a set of stairs looking for an Internet café that turns out to be closed for the holiday. We poke our heads into a music shop next door, which is staffed by a young couple, who are serving one lone male customer, who is very drunk. The boy behind the desk asks if we are American or English. I say "English" and he exclaims, "I love your country, I have your flag, look!" With a beaming smile he points to an old piece of sixties Beatles memorabilia in the form of a Union Jack with the band's name emblazoned across the middle. "I love the Beatles," he adds.

This encourages his drunken customer to approach me, place his heavy, red, mottled face close to mine and, in a gust of vodka-flavoured breath, confide that his four favourite artists are the Beatles, AC-DC, Elton John and ZZ Top, in that order. He goes on to explain in great detail why this is the case, not all of which makes a great deal of sense, then pledges everlasting friendship and bids us farewell with an all-engulfing, malodorous bear hug before making his exit. When we encounter him on the street again fifteen minutes later, our new best friend has forgotten we even exist and lurches past us blindly, ignoring our greetings.

A 2am train departure means a few hours in the dimly lit waiting room of Vladimir station. This consists of a blaring TV set facing rows of metal office chairs, most of which are occupied by the city's homeless and mentally ill who have settled down for the night surrounded by their possessions. Last night, but for the intervention of the taxi driver, this could have been us. Many of the shapeless sleeping forms emit racking, hacking coughs that punctuate the silence every few minutes. There are also a few people, like us, waiting for a train.

The room is presided over by a uniformed female guardian who earlier helped us store our bags in a locked room (the kamera chraneniya) so that we could sightsee around Vladimir unencumbered. However, when we come back a few hours in advance of our train departure to collect the bags she refuses to open the room at first and we are a little disconcerted. It isn't until we take a good look at the waiting room and question her further that we understand that this is because she believes the bags are safer in the lock-up than with us in the waiting room. So, it is best if we leave them there until just before our departure. Actually, although the waiting room looks like a dangerous place to hang out, we conclude in the end that it is safer than it looks. With the tough lady supervisor lady and the police teams patrolling downstairs, it is unlikely that anyone trying to cause trouble would survive very long.

Across the Urals and into Siberia

Where we are seduced by the charms of Russian train life in a universe controlled by provodnitsas.

Our first impression of life on Siberian trains is that it goes by too quickly. We are on train number 10, the Baikal, travelling between Vladimir and Novosibirsk. We have colourful soft bedding, carpeted floors, chemical toilets and a power socket in the cabin. This is one of the top trains on the route and our first class cabin feels first-class. We have stocked up for the 43-hour journey so we don't need the chocolate, fruit juice and cookies that the smiling (yes, smiling!) provodnitsas are peddling down the corridor. Nor are we relying on food from platform sellers, which is just as well as the only thing they are selling at the first major stop we make are teddy bears.

The provodnitsas are the carriage attendants. We have read multiple reports of how strict, unforgiving and domineering they can be. We are not fooled by the cheery demeanour they have shown so far and are suspicious that they are just trying to lull us into a false sense of security. So, we remain resolutely on our guard. Of course, this is completely unnecessary. Throughout our entire journey across Russia the provodnitsas prove to be kind, thoughtful, attentive and extremely hard-working. They don't deserve their reputation as dragons.

Russia passes by the window of our compartment at a steady 50 kms per hour. Forests, rivers and vast meadows stretch to the horizon and occasionally quaint wooden villages or a big, ugly city interrupt the natural flow. We read, snack, doze, listen to music, study Russian and Chinese, chat and pick out things of interest from the endless moving screen of Russian life playing before our eyes. There are churches everywhere and many plots of dachas, country homes for the urban elite, but mostly we just watch people going about their daily business before a backdrop of glorious scenery. The train stop schedule is affixed to the corridor wall so we can see where we will stop and for how long. Train time is always Moscow time, no matter which of Russia's nine time zones we are passing through. This may sound a little strange but the concept works, most of the time. Towards the end of our trip, in the far east of Russia night will fall on the train at a very peculiar hour.

At our second long stop the platform sellers have food: everything from pot noodles to hard-boiled eggs, green salad in plastic containers, chips, sardines, beer, vodka, peanuts, tomatoes, cucumbers and bread. They are also selling bundles of pine branches, small plant pots with white flowers and patterned shawls. This is Balyezino, which means we are thirteen hours into this section of our journey, almost a third of the way to Novosibirsk.

The business on the platform shows all too clearly that these are not tourist trains. They are working trains on working routes. Most of our fellow travellers are Russians going back from the big city, on official business or to visit family. This may explain the excellent trade that the teddy bear sellers enjoyed: selling presents for much-missed children from a long absent father or uncle. As we have seen, these tracks carry enormous freight trains too, some pulling links of wagons hundreds of metres long. After all, the reason the railway line was built in the first place was to bring the produce of resource-rich Siberia to the cities of mineral-hungry European Russia.

At Omsk we encounter the Ulaanbaatar to Moscow train on the other side of the platform. It is breakfast time and Mongolian ladies are at the doors and leaning out of the carriage windows sprinkling food and water from cups and bowls on to the tracks for the spirits of the earth. This land needs all the water it can get. From what we have seen, the countries of Central and Eastern Europe are drying up. The city streets are full of sand and the dust in the air clogs your nose and throat. Although we do not yet know this of course, this desiccated landscape will be with us for the next 12,000 kms until we arrive in Central China.

The route we are travelling was the route taken in 1946 by Sofie's great-grandfather, but in the most different circumstances imaginable. He was arrested in Riga, Latvia in 1944 because he was a member of a pro-independence party, incarcerated in a KGB prison there for two years and then deported to a labour camp in Novosibirsk. He was freed in 1956. His journey in the packed human-cattle wagons carrying tens of thousands of Baltic deportees to the Siberian gulag took over a month with many dying of starvation on the way. (I tell this story in greater detail in the Appendices.)

We cross the Urals in the night and wake up in Siberia. We have passed from Europe into Asia. It has just snowed so we are treated to classic Siberian landscapes, trees and telephone poles frosted with white under the same blue skies that have followed us all along our route so far. As we continue eastwards though, the snow retreats until only small patches remain in tree-covered areas that see no sun.

On the train we are cocooned in our little private space watching the kilometres trundle by. We are extremely relaxed and enjoying the wonderful feeling of having nothing to do. The train stops occasionally but never for very long, as it seems we may be running late and are trying to catch up. Life has a pattern controlled by the provodnitsas who rule over our little universe, regulating lighting, hot water and cabin temperature. They are always busying about, keeping everything spotless. Two provodnitsas operate on long overlapping shifts in each wagon.

A sun the colour of blood orange sets behind us at the end of our first day in Siberia as we gaze out across the Baraba steppe, described variously in guidebooks as "inhospitable" and "Hell in spring." It is nice to be passing through this land on the train, far removed from the clouds of gnats and swampy, almost featureless terrain that has claimed hundreds of lives, many of them prisoners attempting to escape from Stalin's camps.

We doze until the provodnitsa comes to give us the thirty-minute warning for Novosibirsk and as we pull into the station, we dim the lights and look out of our window at the yellow-lit train yard. It is snowing! Our first step off the train and on to Siberian soil is through a crunchy coating of fresh powder.

Novosibirsk and the Altai Mountains

Where we experience legendary Siberian hospitality, go on the least adventurous rafting trip ever and Sofie learns some of the secrets of Banya.

Gleb and Oleg, two people whom we have never met, friends of a friend, are there on the platform at 1.30 in the morning to pick us up, huddled up against the cold and peering out under snow-trimmed hoods. This is our first experience of what we will soon recognise as typical Siberian hospitality, a warmth and generosity of spirit that is all the more impressive given the harsh environment. They drive us to a 70s-era Soviet apartment building and we follow them up the stairway which smells, as we have now come to expect, of concrete dust and urine. However, once they throw open the external iron door to the apartment itself we find ourselves in a cosy, cared for home which, to our amazement, Oleg has vacated for us. He is staying with his girlfriend Svetlana tonight. After effusive thanks from us and instructions from them as to how the water supply and heating system work, they leave us to sleep, which we do immediately. Tomorrow we head south to the Altai Mountains.

We wake yet again to clear blue skies - last night's snow is melting already – and prepare for the trip. We go to a local dive centre near the Novosibirsk railway station to pick up a few bits of gear and fill scuba cylinders. The dive shop owner will be taking a group to Lake Teletskoye this weekend and we will meet him there, as this is our destination too. Teletskoye is the rarely-dived source of the Biya River that courses through the lower Altai to feed the mighty, massive River Ob that divides Novosibirsk and flows on for thousands of kilometres north all the way to the Arctic Ocean. The native name for the lake is Altyn Kyol and the reason that it is so rarely dived is that it is remote. Many are also put off by rumours that the lake contains radioactive wreckage of Soviet space ships that were launched from the nearby (in Siberian terms) Baikonur Space Station in what is now Kazakhstan.

We load our stuff into two 4-wheel drive vehicles and leave for Barnaul in the early afternoon. Once we are out of the city, the road is long and straight. The Russians build roads like the Romans. The further south we travel, the more we see signs of spring in the Altai. The trees that were still bare alongside the train tracks as we came east from the Urals are here budding light green and the light brown taiga is taking on a dark green summer tinge. For kilometre after kilometre we speed towards mountains that we know must lie far in the distance, but all we can see is the flat plain stretching out to an unchanging horizon. Not for the first or last time, our minds are being tricked by the immense scale of Siberia.

We finally come upon the mountains long after night has fallen, having stopped briefly in Barnaul on the way to say hello to Oleg's parents. His father is a retired architect. Both Oleg and Svetlana are architects too, but despite his profession and the family's conspicuous affluence, (the apartment is beautifully decorated), the building it sits in is yet another grey concrete block with the usual odour of construction dust in the lift lobby and bent rusty metal doors. The residents / owners don't seem to feel that maintenance of shared space in a shared building is important.

In honour of Oleg's prodigal return, his mother has been cooking and we sit down to a kitchen table laden with more food than we will ever be able to eat, while the matriarch fusses around her only son and fires off at us a couple of English phrases she remembers from her school days. She is rotund and robust with a classic Russian round pink-cheeked, happy, smiling face framed by blonde curls. Ten minutes before we leave she already has her coat on and her camera primed, ready to accompany us down to the car and take an official photograph to commemorate our visit.

On the road we pass a number of cemeteries. On the train we noticed quite a few cemeteries next to the rail tracks too. At a cursory glance all the graves seem to be of a similar age and it seems strange to us that so many graveyards should be located next to roads and tracks. Probably because we are reading Solzhenitsyn, our minds turn immediately to the labour camps and the slave workers who built – and died building – much of Siberia's road network and the thousands of men and women who died building the Trans-Siberian line.

Perhaps there is a connection. It would be indelicate of us to ask our hosts about this so early in our relationship but at some point we want to find some trace of the labour camps or those who were sent to the camps and stayed in Siberia on their release, unable or unwilling to go home. Perhaps we will find memorials or former camp sites, something to add substance to the trail of Sofie's grandfather.

Svetlana says that she is Siberian but of mixed ancestry, Russian, Polish and Lithuanian. Many Siberians must have a similarly mixed history, given the provenance of most of the people who have come here over the last 300 years: the imprisoned, the deported, the outcast, the desperate and the exiled. On the road to the Altai we see very few Asiatic faces. We spot one roadside shrine to the spirits with colourful rags tied to the bushes and branches around it. Other than that, there is little sign that we are actually in Asia.

We arrive in the pitch-black dark of the early hours and are greeted by the owners of the wooden hut which will act as our Altai base camp. They are introduced as Oleg's old school teacher and her husband. Our first meal there goes on until 3am, brandy instead of vodka, ox-tongue, bread and cheese and Turkish delight. When we wake the next morning, we find that we are in a beautiful valley close to the Katun river, with pine-covered rocky slopes on all sides. A road leads off into purple mountains on the horizon and the whole atmosphere is idyllically rural. Two women are bent over, tending the vegetable patch behind the hut next door, dogs are barking at the chickens and the cockerels are fighting back. Behind a wooden palisade next to the outhouse we can hear pigs snuffling about and sure enough over the palisade is where all the food waste is thrown.

Conversation at dinner last night was largely all about getting acquainted, finding shared interests and telling stories, but we occasionally touch on political and social issues. The gradual disintegration in recent years of the Soviet emphasis on teamwork and collective effort is a strong theme, as is the difficulty that people who live in remote cities like Novosibirsk have in getting visas and other documentation. Everything important needs to be obtained from central offices in Moscow.

After breakfast we drive deeper into the mountains to Chamel and walk along the steep cliffs lining the river Katun, gazing down into the raging white waters. A dam has been built there to control the flood waters from the spring snow melt. The hills are in full purple bloom and we pass a couple of Altai shrines along the path. This is evidently a sacred place.

Orthodox Christianity exists here too, as we discover when we stop in a village to ask the way. A middle-aged woman standing on a street corner is crossing herself repeatedly and muttering under her breath. We pull to a halt next to her. She tells us how to get to the river and asks if we have an icon of local patron Saint Nicholas in the car. We say, "no".

"Well, it's not surprising you got lost then," she replies.

Later in the day we rent a raft and a guide and take to the river, a fabulous vantage point from which to see the cliffs rising on both sides but, perhaps because of the dam further upstream, we don't encounter much white water. The guide tries to introduce some excitement into the occasion by shouting "paddle right" or "paddle left" every time the ultra-calm river threatens to break into a vaguely splashy bit, but we don't fall for it. We have a great time though and take hilarious pictures of us all in our uselessly porous blue one-size-fits-all jumpsuits and equally ill-fitting "safety" helmets.

The evening is taken up by dinner outside in the cold, followed by vodka then Banya, a close relative of the Finnish sauna and a thousand-year-old tradition. The almost mystical quasi-religious esteem in which Russians hold Banya, (to use an article, definite or indefinite, would be to diminish it. The Russians don't.) is hard to understand for those of us who do not have to endure a Siberian winter every year. Oleg tells me that Banya is a key survival technique. It wards off illnesses, maintains the circulation and generally serves to keep mind and body together. He offers to show me secrets of Banya handed down to him over several generations.

Meanwhile Anna offers Sofie a demonstration of her own Banya secrets. This evening, Sofie's reward for having travelled so far is to lie naked in a super-heated wooden shed and be being beaten with birch twigs by a heavily pregnant Russian lady, also naked. That is not something that happens to you every day. I originally join Sofie in the Banya hut but, when we notice that Anna is hovering uncomfortably outside the hot room, still wrapped in her towel, we realise that I have committed a faux pas. So I sidle out awkwardly, leaving the ladies alone. This group seems to have a single sex Banya policy. When I was ice diving in the White Sea last year, it was everyone all in together, male and female, young and old. There is evidently no universal rule.

On the second day we make an early start. At 6.30am there is cloud in the valley and snow has fallen on the hills around us. Apparently, more snow is forecast for later. The plan today is to ride 400 kms into the mountains towards Mongolia along the M52.

As it turns out, the journey will take us through all four seasons of the year in one day and past every type of Alpine scenery imaginable. We will experience frozen rivers, silver-frosted pines, tall snow capped mountains in the distance, green meadows dotted with cows and horses grazing peacefully and villages of mostly wooden houses. We spot local Altai people more and more frequently, the further we go into the mountains. They are the original Turkic inhabitants of the region. Distinctive Mongol faces peer out at us from mud-spattered school bus windows or greet us with welcoming smiles over shop and café counters.

We drive by huge roadside shrines as we crest mountain passes and, at the furthest point of our day's journey, after we have left tarmac roads far behind, we pass a middle aged man and a younger companion riding laden horses up a mountain track. They have the look of men who have come a long way and who still have a long way to go.

In the centre of Aktash, a desolate mountain town, there is what looks like a long-abandoned prison or labour camp. Rows of long low buildings are surrounded by walls with guard towers at the corners and a tall watch tower at the main gate. In the mountains above Aktash an old road leads to a huge red-brown slagheap with rusting mining equipment and overgrown mineshafts all over the surrounding slopes, as well as a small collection of graves dating from the 1950s. Some of the graves are gated, perhaps to protect them from large animals. Others are just marked by plain wooden crosses with no names.

On the way out of Aktash we are zapped by a speed gun and stopped by the DPS-niki, the much derided traffic cops. This is after all the main route south out of Russia and we have seen quite a lot of police activity en route. Oleg, who is driving, is hauled off into the back of the cop car with his documents and ten minutes later he is released, having had to pay a fine amounting to the equivalent of less than US$2. We tell him that is an insult and that the speed he was going deserves a much more impressive fine, but he ignores our demands that he go back and ask the cops for a recount.

The Altai is where the people of Russia's fourth largest city, Novosibirsk, go to play. It is an adventure sports paradise and largely unspoilt, as far as we have seen. From time to time we come upon a clearing in the forest recently denuded of trees and on the road an occasional timber truck lumbers by. But timber trucks are not necessarily evidence of environmental abuse. Most of the houses in the region are built of wood and there is intelligent development going on in various parts of the Altai, mainly to cater to the growing domestic adventure sports tourism market. In fact we have seen no sign of the rape and pillage of natural resources that, we have read, takes place elsewhere in Siberia.

Something we have noticed, especially here, is how many really old vehicles there are still on the roads. These are ancient Soviet-era vans and minibuses, trucks and small passenger cars that make unusual creaking, cranking noises, spew and spit clouds of black smoke and run on completely bald tyres. Yet, somehow, they have survived and still function. Under the rust, dirt and slush they are mostly grey.

Another striking aspect of life in rural Russia is the absence of marketing. Many shops do not have trading names. They just advertise themselves by the product they sell, so a bakery will just have a big sign saying "Bread," for example. Some even just use the word "Magasin (Shop)."

The Turkic-Mongolian people of the Altai take their descent from the Scythians of ancient history and from the Golden Horde, Genghis Khan's Mongol army that crossed these mountains on their way to conquer Europe. At the time of the Bolshevik revolution, when Russia seemed to be on the verge of fragmenting, the Altai people tried to proclaim an independent state called Karakorum, the name of Genghis Khan's original capital city, (which we are destined to visit in a few weeks time.) The Soviet state refused to entertain such a notion and assimilated the Altai Republic by, amongst other things, the forced settlement of Caucasian Russians from the west.

As we have seen, the effectiveness of this process is evident in the paucity of people with Asian features in the lowlands of the Altai. Pale-faced heavy-set Slavs are in the majority, although the Altaisky people still seem to dominate in the highlands.

Teletskoye

Where we scuba dive in a remote mountain lake, have a close encounter with tiny, lethal bugs and discover more Banya secrets.

The snow that fell on our first night in the Altai was apparently winter's last feeble attempt to hold back the advent of the Siberian Spring as we awake on day three in the Altai to glorious sunshine. Today is another early start and another long run southeast from our base camp to Lake Teletskoye.

Oleg has the peculiar habit of warming up the engine of his new-ish Japanese 4 x 4 by leaving it to idle for an hour or so before we set off. Everyone else thinks this is almost certainly unnecessary. Today, having done this, just as everyone is finally on board and ready to go, he puts the over-warmed up car in gear and promptly stalls it. Svetlana shoots him an accusatory stare. In the back, we pretend not to notice.

The early drama is all about the DPS-niki again who first stop us for speeding, then fine us again three minutes later for parking in the wrong place when we stop in Gorno-Altaisk for supplies. It seems they are more active before a holiday and tomorrow is May 9th Victory Day so I guess we are helping to pay for the DPS party. We travel east from Gorno-Altaisk through pastel green meadows lying beneath the pine and silver birch covered slopes of the Altai foothills. The silver birches are everywhere. They fill the plains, cover the mountainsides and line the sky, looking like soldiers marching in single file over the hilltops.

The sight that greets us as we arrive at Teletskoye will rest in the memory forever. The lake stretches out before us with tall cliffs on each side. Trees jut out from the steep slopes right down to the water's edge. The part of the lake that we can see is just the small west to east section that flows into the River Biya. There is much, much more. The huge north to south section that extends to the Chulishman, the main river that fills the lake, begins somewhere over the horizon. We buy a picnic, rent a small motorboat, load the dive gear and head out eastwards. The lake is flat calm and reflects a blue sky sprinkled with white clouds: a scene from a Siberian chocolate box.

The boat is enclosed to protect passengers from the chill wind and eventually we arrive on the east bank where they are building a small tea room. Tourism is still in its infancy here. Few people visited the lake in the past as there was only one tour boat and no infrastructure. The countryside on the east side and beyond through the mountains is a protected wild life reserve and National Park. There are bears, wolves and even snow leopards here, according to our boat driver. There is a village on the north shore to which access is restricted and other than the dirt track that leads there, no roads run beyond Arti Bash, the small town at the northwest corner of the lake, where we will overnight.

Very little reference to this incredibly beautiful part of the world exists on the omniscient Internet in English or Russian and we feel highly privileged to be here. On hearing that we were going to dive Teletskoye, a very experienced and well-travelled Russian diving journalist friend wrote and told us that he was very envious. It had always been his dream to dive the lake.

The tearoom is sort of half open and the lady supervising construction stops one of the carpenters in mid-saw and together they rustle up a mountain of delicious blini with blackcurrant jam. Guided by our hosts we go up the hillside a little way and come across a waterfall surrounded by trees festooned with coloured rags. This is a sacred spring as well as an idyllic retreat.

But once back on the boat, we discover a dark side to paradise. Oleg, who climbed through the woods above the waterfall to take pictures, finds that he has picked up an encephalitis tick, the scourge of the Siberian forests at this time of year. We have been warned about these tiny bugs several times. Their bite is potentially fatal. Oleg's discovery prompts a progressive full body search by Svetlana, which involves him gradually stripping down to his underpants. By the time we arrive at our second stop, she has found a total of twelve ticks. Just in case there are any more of the little beasts hiding away in his less accessible nooks and crevices, Oleg throws himself into the icy two-degree waters of the lake to drown them.

The main reason for this second stop is for Gleb and me to go diving. Unlike Oleg who emerges from the lake tick-free but shivering and a pale shade of blue, we will be using dry suits. We have set up twin independent cylinders, not because we plan a deep dive or a dive with decompression stops, but because of the increased risk of a free-flowing regulator in near frozen water. As we are using rented equipment from the Novosibirsk dive centre, the cylinders and the thermal protection take a little sorting out pre-dive but, once we are underwater, everything works just fine. The huge buoyancy changes that a neoprene dry-suit undergoes on ascent and descent are a surprise at first, as I usually dive with a tri-laminate suit, but it keeps me very warm and absolutely bone dry. The only bits that get cold as usual are my fingers and toes.

We make a beach entry and do a mini exploration of the underside of the cliff next to the beach to a depth of thirty metres. Below ten metres it is completely dark but the water is clear and, with our powerful dive lights, we can see a silty lakebed and a petrified forest of fallen trees and branches populated by small silvery fish skimming through the undergrowth. In one place, a rockslide has created a small weed-covered reef. The temperature sits at 2C throughout the dive and we patrol slowly out and back. All the time, one thought crosses my mind like scrolling headline news. "I am scuba diving in Siberia!" It is quite a thrill.

The post dive ceremony involves a hot glass of tea that Anna brings us as we come up the beach, then a couple of tots of vodka to get the circulation going and a few hunks of bread to soak up the vodka.

When we get back to Arti Bash we move into our new camp, a barracks on the edge of the village, which has been infested with ladybirds and recently sprayed, as we see when we open the door to the sight of thousands of ladybird carcasses littering the floor. The outhouse is located in the backyard at the end of a daunting obstacle course, but is a filthy, smelly, insect infested place so we make a private vow not to use it except in the direst of emergencies.

Fortunately, an option is at hand in the Banya hut across the road right next to the River Biya, just at the point where it emerges from the lake. After stowing all the gear and sweeping up the dead insects, the boys head for Banya first. Oleg introduces me to the ceremony by saying:

"Many things in Russia you just have to feel and once you feel you will understand."

Banya is one of these things. We strip and hit the hot room for ten minutes first, sitting chatting and sweating on our little towels. Then we go back to the cold room for a further ten minutes, have a little tea, kvas, beer or water and then return to the hot room, stoking up the steam and the temperature by throwing water on to the hot stones.

When we can stand it no longer, on a command from Oleg, who is in charge, we leave the hot room at a run, burst out of the back door of the hut and fling ourselves stark naked into the cold, dark river. A little rudimentary pool has been created there so we have some depth and protection from being whisked away downstream by the current. I touch bottom (in the nicest possible way) and swim up into the shallows. I am standing waist deep in liquid ice and steaming gently in the chill night air. My body is pale in the moonlight, my skin tingles from the dramatic temperature shift to which I have just subjected it and I gaze up at a cloudless starlit sky. Not for the first time on this trip, not even for the first time today, I marvel at where we are and how far we have come.

Then it's back into the Banya hut and we repeat the whole process another three times before Oleg calls it a night. Each time we repeat, the temperature in the hot room is ramped up a bit more and the dunk in the river lasts a little longer. At the end, after about an hour and a half, we each fill a plastic bowl with hot water and wash in the outer wet room, between the hot and cold rooms, soaping all over and rinsing with a ladle. We head back to the barracks with minds and bodies purged, feeling relaxed and serene. I must admit that, before, I thought the whole Banya obsession was a little exaggerated but, now, it seems to make perfect sense. Perhaps I am beginning to feel.

On our return, Sofie and the girls go off for their own Banya. It is midnight by the time they finish so we all eat late again tonight, joined by more friends of friends, Andrei, Lena and their two children, who have just arrived from Novosibirsk for the weekend.

Dinner goes on into the early hours and conversation flows freely, as does the vodka. In his book "Into Siberia," Colin Thubron writes about those who lost something when the Soviet Union collapsed, subsequently had difficulty in adjusting to new times and now spoke nostalgically of the Soviet era. Thubron poses the rhetorical question: "when the state has been parenting you for all of your life, what do you do when you find yourself suddenly orphaned?"

But what of the youth of Russia, numerous, educated and hungry for knowledge, for whom the Soviet Union is merely a childhood memory or, for the teenagers of today's Russia, not a memory at all. They look forward, not backwards. They want to travel, create complex lives, develop international Internet communication spaces and, like our travelling companions, bring up children and be free to choose their life paths.

The younger people we have met in Russia talk always of travel. They dream of seeing the world. Destinations such as Bali, Fiji, the Great Barrier Reef, Italy, and Egypt roll off their tongues. Notably, they do not talk of going to America. They do not aspire to be American and we get no impression anywhere that the USA won some sort of spiritual war when the Berlin Wall came down, as many in the West believe. The popularity of McDonalds does not reflect any deep-seated desire to be Western any more than the omnipresence of Sushi bars in Moscow means that many Muscovites want to be Japanese.

The youth of Russia are proud to be Russian, proud of their culture and history. They gripe about their Government just like everybody everywhere. As young urban professionals, in terms of their dreams, aspirations and frustrations, they are no different from their counterparts in London, Rome, Hong Kong or Sydney.

Thubron's pessimism in "Into Siberia" contrasts drastically with the optimism and calm determination to succeed that characterise the Russians we have spoken with. We conclude that many of the folk Thubron interviewed were older and their golden days lay far in the past. It is very difficult in any society to find older people who think that modern life is an improvement on what they experienced when they were younger or who think that today's youth are worthy inheritors of the future. To get an understanding of what is to come, perhaps it is better to talk to those who will be there, who will shape and lead the future. It is unlikely that older people anywhere in the world are a reliable source of information on how younger people view things.

Oleg and Svetlana will redesign their apartment to include a full bathroom with a tub. They plan to fill the bathroom with eco-friendly and ultra-fashionable Lush products as Novosibirsk has a Lush outlet near the main railway station. They explain that their building was originally built in the 1930s when Stalin's Russia was still putting up high quality structures that would last. These apartments were originally built with no inside bathroom. Instead, there was a communal bath-house next to each block. The bathing blocks are long gone.

Although Banya is predominately a rural phenomenon, there are Banya establishments in Siberian cities. However, Oleg describes them as purely functional, primarily constructed for those who have no bathing facilities at home. They are not repositories of the Siberian spirit like the Banya places in the wilderness.

As it is every day, breakfast the next morning is grietski, buckwheat fried in oil. Apparently the word derives from the word for Greece or Greek. Nobody can tell us why. Evidently, this is where folk in the Southern states of the USA got the word "grits" from, though.

Saturday May 9th is a travel day for us, from Lake Teletskoye back to Novosibirsk. It is also Victory Day in Russia, the celebration of the defeat of Nazi Germany in the "Great Patriotic War" in which so many millions of Russians died. Our thirty-something companions have tied orange and black ribbons to their car aerials.

This is apparently a relatively new custom that was not introduced until 2005. Orange and black were the colours of the medal ribbon for the Order of St George, the highest honour that could be awarded in Tsarist Russia and the same colours were used for the Victory Medal in 1945. Black and orange symbolize smoke and fire. Nowadays, on the eve of May 9, people attach ribbons with orange and black stripes to their cars, jackets, backpacks or hospital beds. Many never remove the ribbon for the entire year. The idea is that by displaying the ribbons, the Russian people express their gratitude to those who fought for independence and saved the country from Nazism: the alive and the dead, the known and the unknown.

Military veterans spend May 9th in uniform and don all their medals. They gather with family and friends in public parks and people, even total strangers, come up to them all day to congratulate them, thank them and hand them bunches of flowers. By the end of the day the veterans and their wives look like walking rose bushes.

We are reading "The Gulag Archipelago" as we travel and Solzhenitsyn records a dark side to the victory, that is certainly not celebrated or even mentioned on May 9th. He recounts the story of the treatment meted out to returning Russian prisoners of war after the Nazi defeat in 1945. Solzhenitsyn calculates that many of these men were betrayed not once but three times by the Soviet state for which they fought. They were first betrayed when they were sent out to fight in the early days of the war with inadequate equipment. They were betrayed again after they had been taken prisoner by the Germans, when they were completely ignored by their mother country and left to rot unsupported in the prison camps, as if they were dead already. The third betrayal came in 1945 when the prisoners were repatriated and immediately interned again in the labour camps of the Gulag, because the contact they were assumed to have had with non-Russians in the German prison camps made them politically unreliable.

The returning soldiers were joined in the Siberian labour camps by hundreds of thousands of émigrés who had previously fled the communist government but patriotically (and, as it turned out, unwisely) returned to Mother Russia at war's end. Other new arrivals in the camps were tens of thousands of exiled White Russians who had fought alongside the Western Allies against Nazi Germany and were rewarded for their service after the war by being imprisoned by these same Allies and handed over against their will to the Soviet authorities, who shipped them straight off to the Gulag.

Thus were a huge number of brave, patriotic Russian people, civilians and soldiers, indicted as "traitors of the motherland" and incarcerated in the labour camps of the Siberian Gulag from which many never returned. I wonder if any of those people who have survived to this day celebrate May 9th in quite the same way and for the same reasons. They will be at least in their eighties now. Soon their generation will be no more and their past forgotten: unless, that is, future generations of Russians still read Solzhenitsyn.

We clean up our barracks before we leave and head out of the mountains towards Biisk. Overnight, it seems, carpets of yellow and white flowers have appeared in woods and fields and along the roadside. There is no tarmac on the road to Biisk so for 200 kms we bounce and rattle along, trailing a massive cloud of dust behind us. We pass house after house that already has a mountain of cut wood stacked up in front in preparation for the winter. Our companions remark with wry faces that the Siberian summer is very short. Here and there picnic parties, families, couples or groups of men are sitting around blankets laid on the ground next to battered old Ladas and everyone calls out "Congratulations!" as we pass. We all shout "Congratulations!" back at them, before dousing them with our dust cloud.

Every village we go through is having a party. We see people, some in uniform, dancing in bars and cafes, flags hang over war memorials and the national TV channels are screening war movies all day. We are told that this evening there will be a big Parade of Stars-type variety show on TV and the entire country will come to a halt in order to watch it. This whole day is obviously a major event for old and young.

We try to make it back to Novosibirsk in time for the evening fireworks but, by the time we hit the city, the fireworks are over. Traffic is already pouring back out of town across the main Obb Bridge and people are streaming into the metro stations. (Obviously not everyone is watching the TV show.) We decide to end the day in a smart, fashionable bar appropriately called Victory, next to the city's main cinema complex. Victory has an outdoor terrace with sofas scattered around and, judging from the clientele, it is a favourite haunt of Novosibirsk's young professionals, as well as a selection of heavy-set dudes with appalling haircuts, trying to impress teenage girlfriends with their cosmopolitan sophistication. We order snacks and chat over non-alcoholic lettuce mojitos.

Oleg and Svetlana tell us about the three-door, two spaces concept in the design of Siberian homes. This is a sort of air-lock feature that keeps the cold air out and the warm air in. They also explain why all the common areas in apartment blocks are so poorly maintained. Up until two years ago, maintenance of common areas was the responsibility of the state which, whether through corruption or under-funding, did very little; hence their poor condition. Building residents therefore just concentrated on keeping their own space nice, clean and presentable. Beyond the heavy metal vault doors that guard each apartment the appearance, smell or state of disrepair was someone else's problem. However, two years ago, a law was passed requiring the establishment of building management committees and making each flat owner responsible for a proportional fraction of the building's upkeep.

As we have seen, change has been slow to come. The state is no longer responsible but no-one has assumed responsibility in its place, so the situation has actually gone from bad to worse and the Russians are so used to the situation that they do not really notice. It is interesting that, in the West, where supposedly we are all individuals and there is no collective responsibility, people voluntarily and routinely take care of the area around their houses and jointly look after the common areas of apartment buildings for the general good.

In Russia where the focus is traditionally on the collective, it is every man for himself, at least in this respect. Of course, in the West, community spirit does not exist everywhere and we have our own inner city slums, but the examples we have seen here of despoiled living environments include blocks inhabited by middle class, educated professionals and indeed the whole of Suzdal, supposedly one of Russia's most beautiful towns.

The architects agree and say that the majority of those in their profession find work as interior designers; such is the lack of concern for beautifying external spaces. The exception to this is a project known as Potemkin's Villages, where a lot of effort is made to restore the facades of buildings so that old towns look beautiful for visiting officials and passing tourists. But they are just for show. If you penetrate beyond the facades, you find rubbish-strewn courtyards, walls covered in graffiti and concrete coming off in lumps, exposing the buildings' rusted iron skeletons.

The next day we explore the city of Novosibirsk in sunshine and a balmy temperature of 25 C. The children are playing in the fountains, the parks are full of people dressed for summer and couples patrol the streets hand in hand. We find a wonderful restaurant called Saffron, five minutes walk from the station, that serves fabulous plov and manti. Manti are large steamed meat dumplings, a Kazakh/Uzbek speciality. Then it's time for farewells and leave taking as our carriage awaits.

Irkutsk and Baikal

Where we set up camp on the cliffs above Baikal and dive the world's deepest lake.

That evening at 10.30pm we board train number 8 by walking across the tracks between platforms as the locals do, instead of using the bridge. We have a thirty-hour ride to Irkutsk ahead of us. This is a more basic sleeper than the previous one. As it is not equipped with chemical toilets, we have to put up with toilet closure for half an hour either side of city stops, which always seem to arrive at the wrong time, of course.

We arrive in Irkutsk at dawn, avoiding the trap of getting off the train at the wrong Irkutsk station, (which is seven kilometres before the main station; the train stops there for only two minutes.) Waiting for us at the right station are three girls all named Anna, friends of our travelling and diving partner Gleb. They drive us around Irkutsk, looking for somewhere we can all have breakfast together. We thus have an early opportunity to look at a pretty town with, mercifully, very little in the way of grey Soviet architecture.

Instead there are avenues full of lovely turn of the century buildings in a variety of pastel shades and some beautifully ornate churches. It is a busy city and the hum of traffic starts to build from 7am onwards. Before that we have the roads to ourselves. Eventually, after sitting with us for a bun and a coffee at a fast food joint, the Annas drop us off at the bus station where we pay 100 roubles each for a seat on a 14-passenger minibus for the sixty-minute, sixty-kilometre trip to Listvyanka, the gateway to Baikal. The tickets are cheap but the downside of choosing this form of transportation over a taxi is that we need to be patient. The minibus driver won't leave until he has every seat filled and this takes the best part of an hour. The journey to the lake passes through woodland and skirts a number of smaller lakes until the Angara River appears close to the road on the right side. Shortly afterwards, we enter the outskirts of Listvyanka.

We come upon the lake under a hazy blue sky. A light breeze is rippling its mirror-like surface. The distant hills of the east shore appear as a faint mirage in the haze. Perhaps they are really a mirage and the mind only imagines them, as the eastern shore is fifty kilometres away and the hills are far, far beyond that.

We feel like we have arrived at the edge of an ocean. Listvyanka has the air of a seaside resort on a perfect day in the off season. There is hardly anyone around, just a few local people doing some shopping or sipping coffee outside a café by the pier, which is where the minibus drops us off and sits waiting for passengers for the ride back to Irkutsk. We park ourselves on a bench in the sun to plan our day, and by lucky chance find ourselves close to the cleanest toilets in Russia. They are on the ground floor of a blue five-storey apartment building just off the main street opposite the pier and they are worth every kopeck and more of the ten Roubles entry fee.

The village is peaceful. A dog barks occasionally, breaking the morning calm, and the breeze carries the cries of children playing in a kindergarten somewhere nearby. Fishing boats drift by almost soundlessly, hardly disturbing the surface of the lake with their passage. Midday is approaching, the morning chill has been dissipated by the warmth of the sun. Here at the southern end of Baikal, winter has departed for another year and the thaw is complete. Our timing is perfect.

We stroll down the Listvyanka seafront, have a wonderful lunch, which includes our first taste of the legendary and unique Baikal salmon that they call omul. Then we walk back out of town to the Baikal Museum, where the main draw is an aquarium featuring a variety of Baikal-only species, including two young fresh-water nerpa seals. They are a delight to watch: strange, funny-faced, otherworldly creatures with incredibly streamlined bodies. They are found only in Lake Baikal and one of the museum staff explains that the population numbers around 100,000. Hunting the nerpa is permitted to those with licences and within a tightly proscribed hunting season.

She tells us that hunters kill only 1,000 nerpas a year and that she does not think that this represents a threat to the population. Most of the licensed hunters are men from the indigenous villages on the Eastern (Buryatian) side of the lake. For generations, the villagers there have been using the nerpa to provide them with food, fat and clothing.

It is a great little museum, well worth the detour. There is an enormous stuffed sea-eagle on the third floor and, something very cool, an exhibit in the basement that uses video shot from a bathyscaphe to simulate a voyage in a submarine to the very bottom of Lake Baikal, which is over 1,600 metres deep. You can see that, even at these depths, there is still plenty of life in the lake's heavily oxygenated waters. The exhibit is narrated in both English and Russian by a member of the museum's staff.

We go back into town to pick up some supplies then follow the road north where the village peters out into a small park. We search for what, on the map, looks like a coastal path to Bolshoie

Koty, the next village along the lake. Our idea is to find somewhere off the track but close to shore to put up the tent and camp for the next couple of days. After following a couple of promising tracks that lead only to sheer cliffs, we decide the path is imaginary and abandon the search. Instead, we make our way down to the water, where there is a long stretch of stony beach. The lake is clear and calm; the sky is unbroken blue and we set up a makeshift cooking area, scramble some eggs and boil a kettle of Baikal water to make tea. The sun slowly begins to set behind us but it is still comfortably warm here in Eastern Siberia. No breeze stirs the waters and the only sound we hear is waves gently lapping on the stones at our feet.

By 9pm the sun has gone, the light starts to fade and we move back up the slope to a flat spot overlooking the lake, where we build another fire and pitch the tent. The fire burns too well, so it doesn't last long and the few embers we leave when we finally sleep are unlikely to deter any passing wolves or bears. Just in case we do get any visitors during the night, human or animal, we pack everything into the tent with us, except the food, which we leave under a bush some distance away.

At 10 o'clock exactly the evening warmth evaporates in an instant as an icy wind descends from the north and the temperature drops fifteen degrees in fifteen seconds. The wind blows away the haze over the lake and we can now see the lights of the Buryatian villages on the far bank. We are standing fifty metres above the oldest, deepest body of fresh water on earth, with the endless Siberian forest behind us. Above, wispy trails of cloud now decorate a starlit sky.

Morning arrives early and brings with it the warmth of the sun, encouraging us to doze and sleep in a little. We have a mid-morning cup of tea and then go back down the cliff to the lake side, where our master plan is to hang out on the beach all day and do very little: wash in the clear icy waters, poach some eggs, write a little, read a little, study Chinese, bask in the sunshine and pinch ourselves from time to time to make sure we are not dreaming.

The beach is empty. We saw a small number of visitors in Listvyanka the day before but no-one comes our way today. In the evening the haze clears again and we can see in the distance to the east the white-capped mountains, towards which we will be travelling tomorrow evening. But, before that, we have another night camping, a dive in the lake tomorrow morning with our pal, local dive store owner Gennady Misan, then dinner with the Annas back in Irkutsk.

We really like Listvyanka. The old wooden village lies in the lanes off the main street and the modern beachfront has been tastefully developed. There are no grey, Soviet, concrete hulks here. Instead, plenty of colour, wit, restraint and intelligence have gone into the design of the various projects.

The next morning we dive Baikal. The water is as cold as we expected, one degree colder than Teletskoye and one degree above freezing. We meet up with Gennady and a few of his divers by the shore in the centre of town. He has brought drysuits and full sets of gear for us, including cylinder twin-sets. We swim out on the surface for about 100 metres, looking down at a slowly shelving plateau about five metres below.

Then the bottom drops away sharply into blackness and we descend slowly through the icy water to a sheer wall, covered with green algae and huge green tree-like sponges. The visibility is fifteen to twenty metres and we drift easily along on a slight current. Little fish flit among the undergrowth and occasionally we stop to watch small crustaceans known as gamoros, unique to

Baikal, detach themselves from the wall and swim awkwardly to a new feeding site further on. The gamoros are ancient living fossils, harking back to an age when the most advanced forms of life on earth were the trilobites.

Half-way through the dive, one of our diving companions has a problem when his regulator starts to free-flow uncontrollably. As he is only diving with a single cylinder and the contents of this cylinder are now pouring out rapidly and uselessly into the lake, he has to abort the dive and head slowly but surely for the sanctuary of the surface , taking his dive buddy with him. This is a good reminder of the need always to dive with a substantial back-up air supply in water at this temperature. Thirty minutes into the dive, cold fingers and toes make the warm sunshine on the surface seem very appealing, so we make our ascent and swim back through the shallows to the shore.

Afterwards, over hot chocolate, Gennady tells us more about diving the lake. In March and April, the ice can be up to ten metres thick and, in places, interlocking sheets create a series of ridges and canyons. During this period, you can drive across the surface of the lake in four-wheel-drive vehicles. Where the ice is less thick, holes are drilled and triangular sections of ice are lifted out to give divers access to the lake. When you dive under the ice, it is fascinating to look up and see the magnificent, tortured sculptures on the underside of the surface. There is also plenty of life in the frozen depths. If you are lucky, you may even encounter the nerpa seals. Post-dive, there are Banya huts on the beach nearby to help warm you up again.

You can look for the seals in summer too, when water temperatures reach a balmy 14C. A huge colony is usually found close to an island in mid-Baikal called Yurskani. We immediately set about planning our return.

In the afternoon, Gennady drops us off in Irkutsk and we explore the town on foot for a couple of hours. The sun is beating down on dry, dusty streets full of shoppers. But then, at around 5.30, the weather changes abruptly and a cold gusty wind sweeps in from the north, carrying showers that lay down the dust. We are walking through the park on the south bank of the Angara River when the storm hits and, with no shelter in sight, we just trudge on through it to the Alexander III statue where one of the Annas has said she will meet us.

While we are waiting by the statue in the rain, a couple of police officers beckon us over to a small police post at the corner of the square. Thinking that we are going to get ID-checked we make our way over to them hesitantly, preparing a few quick excuses as we haven't registered our presence in Irkutsk. In fact, we haven't registered our presence anywhere since we left Moscow. However, when we get there we find that they are just inviting us to wait in their office out of the rain. We accept the invitation gratefully and with a tinge of relief. The police post is bare and functional. The only decorations are a photograph of Putin and Medvedev together, an overflowing notice board and a couple of radios hanging on the wall. At the back, there is a small metal-walled cell decorated with the handprints of prisoners-past.

Finally one Anna arrives and takes us to find the other two Annas in a restaurant nearby. There is a sprinkling of customers but the number of diners thins out fast when the live music begins, in the form of an ear-splitting one-man karaoke show. Dinner is fun though and in conversation during the interludes between songs, the Annas tell us how they survive the long winters in Irkutsk when temperatures are often in the minus-30s. Below minus 30C children do not have to go to school.

We tell them how "Siberian" weather in London earlier this year brought a few centimetres of snow and temperatures of minus 7C, which together managed to cause the entire city to grind to a halt. This produces laughter all round. Before, when we related this story to our Novosibirsk friends, Svetlana said she had a girlfriend now living in London who had taken her children to school as normal that day, only to find that they were the only ones who showed up. Of course, none of the other children's mothers was Siberian!

Car driver Anna shows us the remote control for her car, which not only opens the doors but switches the engine on remotely and activates the heater controls. In the morning, she just leans out of her apartment window and points the control at the car several floors below in the car park to get it started and begin the de-icing process. Later, when she is ready to leave for work, she just has to make her way carefully from the front door to the car and she is ready to go. The motor is warmed up, the windows are clear and the passenger compartment is nice and toasty. Modern Siberian survival technology: we are well-impressed.

One of the other Annas helps us clear up a couple of mysteries from our time in the Altai, identifying the ubiquitous purple flowers as rhododendrons and the mine up in the hills above Aktash as a mercury sulphide pit from the 1960s/1970s. Mercury sulphide is used for painting icons and the "gold" domes of orthodox churches. Her knowledge of the Altai comes from time spent on a project in the early 1990s to research the feasibility of installing a hydro-electric power station on the Katun River. The research identified significant potential for environmental damage and the idea was therefore shelved.

Ulan Ude

Where we watch marching bands under Lenin's gaze and visit a Museum of Atheism.

Dinner passes much too quickly and all too soon we are back out in the rain and on our way to the station to catch the overnight sleeper train to Ulan Ude. We thank the Annas for their hospitality and climb aboard. We are in kupe (second class), this time with two lower bunks booked. A couple of Russian businessmen are in the top bunks and a bunch of Russian soldiers in uniform are next door on the other side of the paper-thin compartment wall. They are drunk when we board and seem to be planning on getting more drunk as the evening wears on.

In our compartment we participate watchfully in the etiquette of four strangers preparing themselves for bed in a very confined space, desperate to avoid any faux pas. Everyone studiously tries to ignore what the others are doing, although this is difficult when a total stranger is sitting on your bed taking his trousers off. Access to the upper bunks involves a combination of push up and hop, starting with one foot on each lower bunk, rather like when you pull yourself up and onto the side of a swimming pool.

We will get into Ulan Ude at 6.10am so this is a dusk to dawn ride along the south shore of Baikal. It is not the end of the line by any means as Vladivostok is still thousands of kilometres away but it was actually the last section of the Trans-Siberian railway to be built. In the early days of the line, before this south Baikal section was built, the trains were dismantled on the western side of the lake, taken across by ship and then put together again on the other side.

Before going to sleep I go out into the corridor to charge my phone and get harassed by a couple of the drunken soldiers from the next compartment. They are looking for the provodnitsa but get no reply when they hammer on her door so decide to work out their frustrations on me. One peers down at me aggressively as I sit there and holds his hand out, palm up, as if asking for my papers. I decide to misinterpret the gesture as an offer of friendship and grasp his hand firmly, saying, "my name is Simon, what's yours?" He seems confused and there is an awkward pause while we all wait to see what is going to happen next. Then he mutters, "Yuri" and pulls his hand away. The provodnitsa arrives and I take advantage of this to return to our compartment. It is a short night punctuated at intervals by bouts of heavy snoring from above and next door and ended abruptly by the provodnitsa waking us and demanding her sheets back just after 5am.

We disembark an hour later along with several truckloads of soldiers. They line up and march off and we are left alone on the long platform. It would be dawn if the sun was anywhere to be seen but the sky is low and heavy with black clouds and a light drizzle is falling. Ulan Ude seems an extremely bad place to be on a cold, wet, grey morning but here we are and we don't have a ticket out of here for the next three days.

We trudge off down the platform to a footbridge that seems to lead out of the station. As we head in the direction of what our map tells us should be the town centre, we find ourselves walking through a wasteland of sandy, pot-holed streets. The buildings we pass have their shutters down, the dirty, unpainted concrete walls are pockmarked and we crush fragments of window glass with our boots as we make our way along the pavements.

The only person we see is an old lady who emerges from behind a wall of breezeblocks dragging a large yellow bag. On a whim we take a side road where there is some sign of life, even if this is only a garbage truck reversing, and see a billboard with the word "Geser" stretching across the roof of a three storey grey building. A hotel perhaps? We go up the stairs and push open a door that gives onto an empty corridor. A room off to the left has light coming from it and a girl in a waitress uniform peers out. We say "hotel?" and a female voice from inside the room rings out in English, "ah, you need me!"

By chance, we have stumbled upon an oasis in the Ulan Ude desert. The Geser is just what we need. The lady speaking perfect English is Asian and immaculately turned out at 7 in the morning. She leads us down the corridor, clacking on high heels and turning her head to speak to us as she walks. She books us in efficiently, welcoming us to the Buryatian Republic, offers us breakfast on the house and directs us to our first hotel room since Vladimir nearly two weeks ago.

Not everything is perfect. The room smells of petrol, has a plastic floor and there will be no hot water in the city until tomorrow as the authorities convert the system from winter to summer, whatever that means. So we will have to wait a further twenty-four hours for our much anticipated first hot bath for two weeks. But it is home for now and it feels great to stop moving at last.

The hotel will register our visas so we will have up-to-date immigration papers to show to passport control when we eventually leave Russia. We have been flying below the bureaucratic radar all the way so far. Except for our brief encounter in the rain in Irkutsk yesterday and the mini-fines extorted from us by the traffic cops in the Altai, we have had no contact with officialdom at all. Everything we have read suggests that travelling freely and independently like this through Russia was impossible until quite recently.

While we are in reflective mood, we realise that the rain that fell on us in Irkutsk last night was the first we have seen since leaving England six weeks ago. As we lie on the bed in our little gasoline-scented room with the windows wide open to help us avoid asphyxiation, the sky above Ulan Ude still weighs down heavily and occasional long gusts of Siberian wind fill the net curtains. In spite of the ominous weather and our gloomy first impressions of the town when we arrived, we are looking forward to exploring Ulan Ude.

After a short nap, we wander around the streets of the town centre, which has now woken up. The large number of Asian faces among the shoppers shows how close we are to Mongolia and how little progress Caucasian colonists have made here compared with the other parts of Siberia we have seen. We walk past Ulan Ude's most notorious landmark, an incongruously huge Lenin's head statue with almond eyes. Perhaps the sculptor wanted to suggest mischievously that the great man had Eastern origins. (He didn't.)

The wind is icy and we escape into a local restaurant where we warm ourselves up with pelmeni and omul, washed down with cranberry mors and kvas, before venturing out again to people-watch. The weather seems to have relaxed its grip on Ulan Ude and a little blue sky is showing above the mish-mash of immediately forgettable, squat, featureless buildings that make up the town centre.

The city streets are even more dangerous here than elsewhere in Russia, with bus drivers openly intimidating pedestrians who don't scuttle quickly enough across the faded paint of the crossing points. Everyone drives at one of two speeds, 100 km/h or stop.

We do some food shopping, again marvelling at how little merchandising is done here to try to tempt shoppers into buying. Teenagers and twenty-somethings adopt a wide variety of styles of dress and the cultural confusion is emphasised by a group of marching bands rehearsing on the main square, featuring baton-twirling majorettes in knee-length white boots and mini-skirts and dark-skinned Buryats playing trombones, trumpets and a tuba. We go back to our room early to recharge our batteries for tomorrow and relax in front of the Chinese ethnic-Mongolian TV channel to get us in the mood for the next part of our trip.

Day two in Ulan Ude starts with music and dance. We go back into town to start exploring again and see that the main square in front of Lenin's Head has been police-fenced off and a big poster board has been erected next to the statue announcing an "International Marching Band" contest. Aha, now we know what yesterday's display in the square was all about. A few onlookers have gathered and a couple of buses behind the square are disgorging majorettes, musicians young and old carrying brass instruments and a troupe of dancers in what we take to be traditional Buryatian dress.

A few minutes later, the crowd has grown. VIPs, (we assume) have taken their places on rows of plastic chairs set up inside the cordon on the street-side of the square and martial music blares from loudspeakers. A couple of presenters, one man, one woman, prattle through the introductions and then the whole thing kicks off. The bands and majorettes all march on to the square together. Then everyone lines up in formation. There is a strip of carpet extending from the VIP seats to a wooden box that has been placed in the centre of the square. A short, white-haired man in white shoes and an awful white suit two sizes too big for him marches on importantly, climbs on to the box and raises both hands to signal the massed bands to start the opening number together. As he conducts, he is assisted by three other guys who are keeping time with big heavy sticks enthusiastically, but, sadly, not simultaneously. Two of them are following what is apparently the latest Ulan Ude fashion trend and are also wearing dreadful over-sized suits and white shoes. The third probably didn't have time to change.

It is a bizarre scene, especially given where we are on the planet. If you close your eyes to the massive Lenin's Head that dominates the square, you could be watching bands playing at a village fete in England or a Thanksgiving Parade in a small town in the USA. But this is Ulan Ude, capital city of the Buryatian Republic in eastern Siberia!

The massed bands eventually march off to rest before their individual performances and the folk in national costume take centre stage. They turn out to be a dance troupe and they steal the show. They are colourful, lively and witty, even using the old shtick routine of one dancer falling over then running around wildly to try to find his place in the formation again. We laugh along with everyone else. In fact, the whole audience is rolling in the aisles – it's sensational stuff.

Sadly, the same cannot be said of the marching bands that follow them, who take themselves very seriously but are substantially less than sensational. They are still quite entertaining, though. If you have ever watched a marching band anywhere in the world, you can picture the scene. All the clichés are here: over-enthusiastic band leaders seizing their big moment; majorettes desperately trying to keep their thigh-boots in step but failing; reluctant teenage boys shuffling along behind them, peeking at the girls through hair which falls out from under the caps and over their eyes; smaller lads in over-sized uniforms and caps, bored and distracted.

To add another ingredient of farce to proceedings, the enormous sign advertising the contest, set up next to Lenin's Head, collapses in a gust of Siberian wind. It starts blowing across the square, taking its guy ropes with it, along with a couple of workmen, who are hanging on bravely, trying to slow it down. The whole event is very small-town, but it has drawn a crowd of about 1,000 away from Saturday lunch-time shopping so one imagines the organisers will be happy. For us, it is a sheer delight: a wonderful and completely unexpected treat.

If we are probably the only foreigners in the crowd on the square for the marching bands, we are certainly the only visitors to the History Museum later that afternoon. We push the main door open and the building caretaker rings for a girl to open the cash desk to take our money. He then makes a second phone call and motions us upstairs with a smile. At the top of four flights, we encounter a lady curator who greets us courteously and unlocks the first of four exhibit rooms on three levels, each of which she locks up again carefully when we come out. Then she leads us off to the next room. The highlight is an astonishing collection of Buddhist artefacts, which was saved from destruction by a group of devotees. In a masterpiece of deception, they somehow managed to convince the Soviet authorities that, instead of being destroyed, the artefacts should be housed in a "Museum of Atheism," established for educational purposes. This then became the History Museum when the Soviet Union collapsed.

Leaving the museum we cross town to try to find a Chinese restaurant that we have read is very good. We stroll along streets and paths covered in sand, between blocks of quaint old wooden houses with decorated shutters and eaves. Dry air and dusty streets have been a feature of every town we have visited on this journey. There seem to be no restaurants at all in the area and we are about to give up on the place, when suddenly we spy it, nestled between two large, deserted construction sites. Unlike many of the places we have looked for after reading directions in guidebooks, this one is actually there!

After lunch, a passer-by is highly amused by the fact that we are taking photos of the little Korean-made minibuses in Ulan Ude bus station. For him, it is evidently normal to see cars with patterned leather panels on the OUTSIDE, on the bonnet in front of the windscreen. For us it is new, weird, inexplicable and definitely worthy of a picture or two.

Back in the town centre, we find a small children's fun-fair featuring rides with themes such as Red Indians, Pirate Ships and Asterix and Obelix. We guess these were bought second-hand from Europe and transported here. It is hard to imagine what cultural references such as these might mean to Siberian under-5s.

In the evening we are back in our room watching local television and see that it is Eurovision day in Russia. As we are five hours ahead of Moscow time the marathon music-fest itself will not be shown here until the early hours of tomorrow morning so all we get is the build-up. We switch off after a while. We are not that interested in seeing if Lord Lloyd Webber can carry Britain to Euro glory for the first time in decades. As it turns out, he doesn't.

We noticed today on the streets of Ulan Ude that, although there are many more ethnic Asian people here than anywhere else we have been in Siberia, the white Caucasian Russians and Buryats do not seem to mix socially. This observation is based solely on what we saw during the few hours we spent walking around the town centre today but the segregation was noticeable, and it was not something we were looking for. Only in the case of the children playing football or hanging out in the wasteland between apartment blocks did there seem to be no divide. Maybe we should have expected it. This is something of a colony after all and perhaps it is unsurprising that the two sectors of the population should have little in common. I think of 20th century Hong Kong as another example where the same was true.

The Route out of Russia

Where our cabin is invaded by smugglers and we get hauled off the train at midnight.

The next morning we leave Russia with mixed emotions. During the last three weeks or so we have met some wonderful people, seen some truly incredible places and travelled independently with a minimum of difficulty through a country of vast contradictions.

The platform at Ulan Ude is heaving with shoppers and traders as we board the train. Unlike at previous stops across Siberia, where locals were selling to travellers, here the traders are Mongolians travelling home and the shoppers are the folk of Ulan Ude grabbing a quick bargain during this thirty-minute window of opportunity. There are only two trains per week that pass through the city en route between Ulaanbaatar and Moscow, so this is something of an event. The stop is too short for all the shopping and negotiating that needs to take place and, as we pull out of the station, we see one trader literally selling the leather jacket off his back before sprinting for the carriage door, where his pals are hanging out to pull him on board. Our last glimpse of the people of Ulan Ude is of them clambering back over the tracks to the station concourse, clutching their new handbags, jeans and t-shirts.

We look around us and, for the first time in Russia, we have other foreign travellers in our wagon, albeit few. The other thing we notice, to our delight after our recent kupe experience, is that the walls in SV (first class) are much thicker and better sound-proofed. This is another good reason to splash out the extra cash.

We are in the back of the train and, going south from Ulan Ude, we get some great views of the front few carriages as we snake along the course of the Selenga River. Very soon we are crossing the grassland of the steppe but again it is very dry and sandy. It feels like we are on the fringes of the desert already but we will not actually come to the edge of Gobi for another 24 hours. We will follow this river all the way into Mongolia and, as we rumble slowly along, the view is peacefully pastoral, with occasional wooden villages and fishermen waving to us from small boats. A photographic highlight is Goose Lake, about half way to the border, although an enormous ugly factory complex just to the south of the lake mars the spectacular landscape.

We arrive at Russian border control at Naushki bang on schedule, of course, and prepare ourselves for a long wait while everybody is processed. Three hours is the norm, apparently. Our passports are taken away and we are relieved of our most recent visitor registration forms by a separate official. It was such a good idea to stay in a hotel for our last couple of nights in the country so that we had these papers. A few black market currency traders move along the corridors selling Mongolian togrog but the traders look decidedly dodgy so we decide to wait and choose the safer option of a bank when we get to Ulaanbaatar.

We are stationary at Russian border control for just a shade under five hours. The stop includes a full physical search of every cavity of the train accompanied by a lot of shouting. It is dark by the time our passports are returned and the officials disembark. We pull away slowly into the fenced off no-man's-land between Russia and Mongolia and there is suddenly a burst of frenetic activity from the traders who, with the help of the provodnitsas, start moving hundreds of cardboard boxes, bags and bulging pillowcases into our wagon. They pull up the corridor carpets and start piling boxes into hidden storage holes in the floor beneath. In the cabins, including ours, secret panels in the ceiling are pulled open and more boxes crammed in. Nobody asks our permission to do this and we just watch them dumbfounded, shocked and more than a little apprehensive. What if the cabin is searched and the authorities think all this stuff is ours?

The train grinds to a halt in the darkness just beyond the floodlit fence-line for a few minutes, perhaps to give everyone more time to hide everything before we reach the Mongolian Border Control Point. It certainly seems that way because, as soon as the last bit of carpet has been replaced neatly, the train lurches off again and two minutes later we pull into Sukhbaatar. As it turns out, to our considerable relief, there is no physical check of the first-class compartments by Mongolian customs officers. The traders and provodnitsas evidently knew this would be the case. Customs declaration forms are handed out. We complete them but they are not even collected.

Pre-trip research suggested that, as the holder of a Hong Kong Identity Card, I would be permitted to enter Mongolia visa-free, but the police officer who comes to the cabin to check our passports and visas evidently finds this notion humorous. He points at my face and says "you not Chinese" then hauls me off the train and takes me to his chief's office. The chief is a heavy-set guy in a light grey suit who sits marooned on a little furniture island in the centre of a small office that is being painted. He hears my story, tells me not to touch the walls and explains that I need to buy a visa. He pulls a book of visas from his safe and takes a form from the desk drawer. In between questions, I look around the office. A notice board contains one item, an FBI Most Wanted poster for Osama Bin Laden. Once he has finished, he sends me back to the train, which is sitting engine-less for some reason and guarded by a couple of bored-looking uniformed soldiers.

§2

Mongolia

Mandalgobi

Where we start to learn Mongolian ways, breakfast above the poo stratum, slurp mutton noodle soup at midnight and start the day on a bottle of vodka.

We wake early to an alien world. We are surrounded by bright green, tree-less, rolling hills dotted with little round white tents here and there and the occasional neatly-fenced, wooden village, under the blue-est of blue skies. This is Mongolia and this will be our home for the next ten days. Just before we arrive in Ulaanbaatar, as usual the provodnitsas whip away our sheets and return the tickets that they have been holding hostage.

On the Ulaanbaatar platform we eventually track down Tsetsegee, a lady whom we met online and who has arranged an old beaten up Soviet van for our trip, together with a driver, a translator and, although we did not ask for one, a cook. The van is a Ouaz Furgon, built in a factory in Minsk and a common sight rattling down the roads everywhere in Siberia. The Ouaz Furgon rides high off the road, has no creature comforts and its design owes nothing to style or beauty. But they are said to be highly reliable vehicles and fixable everywhere. In the Gobi, where we are going, we guess these are the most important qualities a car should have.

It could have been much, much worse. As we pull away we see four other newly arrived tourists pushing their tour van out of the station car park with their guide shouting at them from the driving seat.

The cook turns out to be one of the Tsetsegee's English language students, whom she is grooming to be a "guide", which is what they call the translators. The real guide is the driver, who is the only one who knows where we are going. He just uses the translator to communicate with us.

Our first stop is at the bank where we change a little Western currency for a lot of Togrog, then we head for a petrol station to fill up the van, along with two jerry cans and a spare fuel tank which lives beneath our seat in the back. Gas stations will be few and far between from here on. We drive out through the suburbs of the city and as soon as we pass the "Welcome to Ulaanbaatar" sign, the tarmac ends and we swing off across the countryside, heading south through the road-less grasslands of Central Mongolia. It feels like a different planet and, for much of the time on this trip, we will be the only inhabitants. When we were planning the journey, we had great difficulty finding a van and driver, as we were visiting "out of season." We will not meet many fellow travellers over the next few days.

Soon after leaving the city, we circle around for a couple of minutes and finally come to a halt for breakfast. On getting out of the van we discover that we have stopped in the middle of a grassy plain covered in animal droppings. At first we are perplexed as to why the driver should have chosen this particular spot, but after walking around a little, while the cook is preparing our food, we conclude that the whole area is covered in goat poo and we must have been circling to find a relatively lightly covered patch. Our team has foreseen this minor problem, however, and a foldaway table and five stools are produced from the back of the van, so we can eat a few centimetres above the poo stratum.

The scenery as we continue south feels like the world of Mad Max crossed with Star Wars. To our surprise, it turns out we are on safari. White-tailed gazelle chase each other across our path, we spot marmot scuttling away across the rocks and, when we stop to explore the ruins of an old temple destroyed by the Stalinists of the Mongolian KGB in the 1930s, we see a pair of ibex perching regally on the cliff.

We are a disruptive influence. A variety of small rodents scuttle back into their holes as we pass and birds are roused from their nests in the short grass by our approach. We rattle and roar past goat herders on horseback, groups of scruffy camels shedding their winter coats and the occasional isolated ger homestead, where women at work and children playing in the sand outside the round felt tents stare at us impassively, ignoring our waved greetings. We feel like invaders.

We stop for lunch at a trackside ger, which doubles as a truck-stop café catering to passing travellers. Needless to say we are the only customers. The milk is on the boil when we arrive and very tasty it is too. Then a man comes in carrying half a freshly-skinned goat over his shoulder and deposits it on one of the three beds in the ger. We are seated on the other two beds. It says much for our experiences over the last few weeks that this does not even cause us to raise an eyebrow.

It seems a bed in a Mongolian ger can have multiple uses. It can function as a seat, a table, a storage cupboard or even as a food preparation area, as we see here when one of the women cooking our food sits down next to the goat and starts slicing pieces off to add to our noodles, which are frying in a wok on the central stove. The cooking fuel is dried animal dung, which is kept in a large can beside the stove. I think the noodles and fresh goat are delicious, although Sofie disagrees. As we leave we see the skin of the goat we have just eaten drying out in the sun on a nearby wall.

Seating arrangements are, driver and cook in the front, translator, petrol and us in the back. The translator bombards us with questions both expected, such as "what music do you like?" or "where do you live?" and unexpected, such as "what are your politics?", "what do you think of Winston Churchill?" and "euthanasia, good thing or bad thing?" It is hard to concentrate on formulating educated, considered replies when you are being thrown around the back of a van, bumping and swerving across the savannah.

The conversation takes a noteworthy twist at one point as it turns out that one of the most popular TV shows in Mongolia at the moment is "Britain's Got Talent." Having been in Russia for most of the last month, we are not up to date so cannot really join in, but we find it surprising that a show which seems so parochial can strike such a chord in people from a wildly different culture on the other side of the globe. The producers evidently have a cross-cultural goldmine on their hands.

We end the day at Mandalgobi, a shantytown in a Gobi valley, which turns out to be the driver's home town. Everyone is going to bunk down for the night in the driver's brother's house, all seven of us in the one room, including the brother and his wife. We are offered the two beds and accept. The toilet is a small hut in the corner of the yard furnished with two planks of wood above a gaping pit. The lady of the house warns us that it will be very dark in this corner later and advises that if we get the call of nature during the night we should not risk falling into the pit but just do whatever we have to do in the yard. We glance at each other with a look that says, no matter how desperate we are, we are not going to go to the toilet in our host's garden.

We start to settle down for bed at around 11 but the brother's wife has not finished with us yet and, to our dismay, won't let any of us sleep until we have had one more bowl of mutton noodle soup. The room fills with the sound of slurping and the smell of boiled sheep fat. The driver and his brother are absent, having made their escape to whatever is the local equivalent of the pub.

I don't know what she put in the mutton soup, but that night I have wild kaleidoscopic dreams. I have been reading in one of the guides that you can find brown, blue and red cashmere goats in the South Gobi. In my dreams, I see squid of different colours that, instead of spraying ink, eject cashmere thread when frightened, which then congeals into fully formed clothing. That's freaky, man!

At breakfast there is the usual symphony of slurping and throat clearing. There is also much sighing and gasping as every mouthful taken is accompanied by a noisy intake of air. We set off at 9 but stop again almost immediately for a vodka break with an old school friend of the driver's, who is waiting for us by the track just out of town for a quick heart-starter. The friend shows us his official government ID and we all make the required noises to show how impressed we are. He then produces a bottle of local vodka and passes it around. I admire his flash new Japanese 4 x 4 and he dismisses the compliment, saying that this is the worst of his many cars and he has much nicer cars at home. A couple of rounds later, the vodka is finished, so he bids us farewell and off we go again.

The landscape now consists of nothing more than a plateau of stones and scrub. Occasional groups of hairy, twin-humped camels ignore us as we speed by. By the time we stop for lunch on the cliffs above Tsong Ovoo we are on Mars, surrounded by nothing but pebbles and sand with the unrelenting wind creating little tornados all around us and threatening to dismantle our cooking tent. Sand is everywhere, inside the van, inside our luggage, up our noses, in our ears, everywhere.

When we start off again, the seating plan in the car has changed and we now have the cook next to us. He has his English phrasebook to hand and his strategy seems to be to use this to prepare a question for us in his head, spend a few minutes memorising it and then let fly. "Are you interested in your country's educational system?" is a typical example. Sadly, he is not prepared for a response so just looks blank when we try to give him an answer. Eventually, he runs out of questions and the van falls silent. The peace is broken by the translator who suggests a game of "I Spy". His timing is perfect - we are now well and truly surrounded by nothingness. This is going to be the easiest game of "I Spy" ever.

We have had Mongolian folk music on the cassette player all morning, which sounds a lot like Chinese opera. We have also discussed families. The translator's grandmother, who is now 85, has a total of over 200 children, grandchildren and great - grandchildren. If this is true, then given that the population of the entire country only numbers around two million, she is responsible for quite a significant percentage – a super-granny!

Across the Gobi

Where we are buffeted by Gobi winds, visit a glacier in the desert and learn more than we ever wanted to about killing a sheep.

Our journey the following day takes us towards the mountains that fringe the Mongolian Gobi to the south. We pass a number of remote ger settlements and, as dusk is falling, we swerve away from the dry river bed that we have been using as a road and climb into a patch of low rolling hills that lie beneath the mountains, looking for a place to pitch the tents.

When we finally stop and emerge from the van, stretching our aching limbs and rattled bones, we find that the warm, sand-filled wind that has been with us all day has turned into an icy, sand-filled wind that is gusting ferociously and seems to come from all directions at the same time. In the absence of any foliage it is impossible to see the wind, it just IS. It is a force of nature that, no matter where we try to put up the tents, we cannot escape from. We erect our little tent on a gentle slope and surround it with rocks, not only to help hold it down should the wind increase in force still further during the night, but also to try to prevent our accident prone translator from walking too close and tripping over the guy ropes again. He has done this three times already. He is a city boy and seems completely out of his element out here in the wilderness.

By the time we eat, it is freezing cold and the hot food loses its warmth almost immediately, leaving us with cold vegetable soup and grits. With no meat on the menu, the driver is not interested in eating and has retired to his nest in the back of the van. He mutters something as he leaves and we ask the translator what he said.

"Meat is for men, grass is for animals," is the answer.

We go to bed soon afterwards. We are cosy in the tent with our thermals, our silk liners and sleeping bags but the noise of the incessant wind trying to uproot us and carry us over the plain is intense and growing louder all the time.

Despite our efforts to seal all the vents, the wind brings sand into the tent and later in the night, having finally fallen asleep, I wake around 4am to feel a fine dribble of sand falling on my face via a flap that has come unsealed. I reseal it and, in doing so, manage to release a small dune that has built up in a crease. It falls unerringly straight into my mouth. I scramble out of the tent to spit and irrigate my mouth with our valuable, limited, drinking water supply. If anything, the wind has become even stronger and some of the gusts produce a deafening crescendo of whistling and roaring and cracking. As the wind makes it difficult to stand, I crawl around the outside of the tent on my hands and knees checking the ropes. All are holding fine. The bark of the Gobi, at least on this night, is worse than its bite.

We wake again just after dawn to a light rain and low cloud obscuring the mountains. After a wash with water from the shower bag hung on the back door of the van and a quick breakfast, we drive off to the Yolyn Am valley where the plan is to hike five kilometres into the centre of the mountains to visit a frozen river held captive and sunless in a narrow canyon between tall cliffs.

When we get there it is quite a sight, ice several metres thick covering a stream of clear water. The sand and dust storms have taken their toll on the glacier and the green and white of the icepack is pockmarked with patches of brown. Winter in the Gobi is long gone and the ice is melting in places but, even at the height of summer when the temperatures are frying the desert beyond the mountains, the glacier never disappears completely.

As we stroll through the valley leading to the canyon we see a variety of rodents, hamsters, voles, jerboa and mice scampering for their burrows. These are everywhere, the area around our camp-site last night looked like brown Swiss cheese.

At the mouth of the canyon there is a wooden hut which contains a tiny museum displaying some scraggy looking stuffed animals and animal skins, as well as some dinosaur eggs and fossilized bones, reminding us that Mongolia lies second in the list of countries ranked in order of the number of species of dinosaur discovered. This is in spite of the fact that, for seventy years of the last century, during the Soviet era, no paleontological research took place in the country at all.

As we leave Yolyn Am and head west towards the sand dunes 200 kilometres away we pass a fairly large flock of sheep and goats being tended by two little girls who cannot be more than five years old respectively. We query this and the translator replies that this is normal in Mongolia, where children are given and learn to take responsibility at an early age. We are impressed. We tell him that children of this age in the West have trouble looking after their own noses, let alone a herd of animals all alone in the wild expanse of the Gobi.

We drive on and reflect on how incredibly harsh the environment is here. Temperatures reach 40C in summer and minus 20C in winter, when the Gobi is snowbound. Spring is the harshest of all seasons and is a time of wild climactic fluctuation, as we have already experienced. Yesterday's stifling heat has been replaced by near freezing cold today. The air is dry; a light drizzle this morning notwithstanding. The real rain comes in late summer when the Gobi turns bright green.

We stop for lunch on the plain and the cooking tent goes up again to protect the stove from the constant, unrelenting wind. It is an eerie sensation that we just cannot get used to. With no trees or bushes you can't see the wind, you can just feel it and hear it. The driver uses the break to clean his windows and mirrors. The van is his world and he looks after it well. The milometer is showing 54,000 kms, probably not for the first time. We will be doing 2,000 kms this week alone and the driver has owned the vehicle from new for about ten years.

From our picnic spot, we look to the horizon in all directions and see nothing but rock and sand. However, despite all appearances, we are not alone. A woman emerges, as if from nowhere, driving a herd of goats. We walk over in the direction she came from, nodding a greeting as we pass, and climb to the brow of a small rise. On the other side is a solitary ger with a grey stone animal pen next to it. It is something we have commented on a few times over the last couple of days. You think you are the only living beings for miles around and then someone suddenly appears out of the brown and blue nothing. It may be a child on a bicycle, a man on horseback or three people squatting next to the track fixing a motorbike. They are tiny islands of life in a sea of emptiness.

Without any prompting, our translator decides to entertain us with a lengthy description of how sheep and cows are slaughtered here in Mongolia. Briefly, cows are killed with a blow between the eyes with the blunt end of an axe. We probably could have guessed that. You kill a sheep, however, by slitting open the chest, reaching inside and then either compressing the windpipe or ripping out the carotid artery with your hand. We certainly wouldn't have guessed that.

Killing the sheep in this way supposedly causes it no suffering. However, the process requires a number of assistants to hold the animal down, (which tends to contradict the theory that no suffering is involved.) The translator goes on to tell us that the head of the sheep is considered a great delicacy when skinned and boiled and the sheep's palette is particularly favoured by Mongolian women.

Having noticed apparent suicidal tendencies on the part of a number of goats we have seen over the last couple of days, we ask what happens if you are driving and hit and kill a goat. Apparently, the going rate is 80,000 Togrog (about US$30). To put that in perspective, the average monthly wage in Ulaanbaatar is around US$100.

We have noticed a strange visual trick that the Gobi plays on you. When you look far into the distance, the plain on all sides seems to be a lush, verdant lawn while, where you stand, the ground is stony and dotted with only odd clumps of thin wild grass. So you walk towards the green carpet but it just recedes as you approach and the thin, comparatively bare ground beneath your feet never changes. It seems that your eyes compress the distance to the far horizon, making all the occasional clumps of grass look like they are growing together side by side. We saw a similar phenomenon from the train in Siberia where small copses of silver birch trees hundreds of metres apart seemed to form a forest on the horizon; a horizon that you could spend your life walking towards but never reach, as many of those attempting to escape from the Gulag discovered to their cost.

As we continue westwards, we see the start of a long line of dunes beneath the mountains to the south of us. A small forest of yellow, spiny, sharp-leafed plants comes and goes. The track has become completely indistinguishable from the surrounding plain. We are travelling between two mountain ranges. Those to the north are glowing red in the late afternoon sun. Those to the south are stony grey, the sand dunes beneath them looming larger as we approach and casting deep shadows. The cook, who is also experiencing this incredible scenery for the first time, is wide-eyed with wonder; "I am proud of Mongolia," he exclaims.

Highlights of today's drive include finding a goat all on her own in the vastness of the desert, licking the afterbirth from a new-born kid. The umbilical cord is still dangling behind her and she looks understandably anxious as we approach to take photographs, although we move slowly trying not to disturb her. She still doesn't trust us and, at her urging, just a few minutes old, the kid lurches with difficulty to its feet and stumbles after its mother.

Tonight we are staying in a ger belonging to a family who live at the edge of the dunes with two dozen camels, a couple of the friendliest dogs in the world and about a million goats. Animals and people live together amid the ocean of droppings. Proud possessions, lying inside against the wall of the ger or tucked behind one of the 81 roof spokes, include an ornate saddle, a rifle and a TV remote control. We count the spokes because we have read that the number 81 is a standard and signifies something important. As we travel on, we conclude that this is not the case. We never find a ger with the same number of roof spokes as any of the others.

All gers face south, "to watch for the threat from China" according to our translator, who seems to prefer Mongolia's northern neighbour. "The Russians are our brothers," he announces frequently. We wonder if all Mongolian 21 year olds share this view. When I told him that Hong Kong people would be very interested in visiting Mongolia and that Hong Kong might be a profitable tourist market for Mongolians to pursue, he is not keen. "Chinese!" he says dismissively.

He tells us that Russian President Vladimir Putin recently visited Mongolia and that children can choose between studying Russian and English in school, but not Chinese.

Indeed, the fact that Mongolia even still exists as a country is unlikely, given its position, sandwiched between two huge powerful neighbours, both of which have munched away at Mongolian territory over the centuries and have notorious precedents for occupying other countries and then subsuming their people and cultures into the whole so that they disappear as individual entities.

The history is complex, of course. One of the greatest Chinese imperial dynasties, the Yuan, was actually Mongol. It was established by Genghis Khan's grandson, Kubilai, with his grandfather as the founding entity, and ruled over most of what we now know as China.

Citing this historical precedent, Mongolia was later "re-assimilated" by the Manchu Qing Dynasty. It was not until the Qing fell in 1911 that, with Russian help, present day Mongolia recovered its independence, albeit in geographically truncated form. China still held on to the lion's share of former Mongolian territory to the south, however, which explains why an overwhelming majority of the world's seven million Mongol speakers live in China today. Neither, however, did Russia return northern Mongolian lands such as the Buryatian Republic that it had seized over the centuries.

Subsequently, Mongolia's strong ties with the Soviet Union, and the difficult courtship between Beijing and Moscow that characterised the early decades of the communist era, meant that China did not recover her "lost" territories when she recovered her strength after 1949.

There is every reason to suppose that our translator and many of his countrymen view China as the major threat to Mongolian independence and nationhood and that they see relations with their Russian "brothers" as crucial to preserving the status quo.

It is striking that everyone you speak to stresses the Mongolian nature of everything around them, even trivial things that have no particular Mongolian connection. For instance, they may talk about drinking Mongolian water out of Mongolian glasses. It is almost as if their continued existence as a nation depends on the constant reassertion of their independence and individuality.

South Gobi

Where we herd goats on camel-back, find out that we have inferior teeth and help our hosts with their TV reception problems.

We emerge from our ger to a view of blue sky over the dunes and mountains of the south Gobi. After breakfast we take some of our host's camels and ride out to the dunes with his teenage son as guide. Many of the camels we have seen so far on the trip look as if they are shedding their winter coats. Some have also been sheared and are naked of fur from the humps down. The camels we are riding are similarly dishevelled, although their haughtiness and air of superiority suggest that they are unaware that they just look like tatty carpets on legs.

It takes us just over an hour to reach the dunes. They are much further away than they look, another Gobi trompe l'oeil effect, and as we approach we begin to appreciate just how huge they really are. We hobble the camels at the foot of the first dune and start climbing the slope, heading for the highest ridge. It is hard work and of course, with the length of time it took us to get here, we are climbing during the hottest part of the day. However, the view from the top is well worth the considerable effort. The monolithic yellow seascape of dunes stretches out to the horizon to both east and west and contrasts sharply with the battleship grey of the fringing mountains to the south.

The Gobi is truly beautiful, a wilderness of contrasts and extremes. The scale is immense. Our ger is a tiny white dot to the north of us and our camels are small dark figures far below. A gale is blowing over the ridge and we are getting heavily sand-spattered, so we decide to head on back. Sliding down is much quicker than stumbling up and very soon we have remounted our camels for the journey home. On the way, our host's son says he wants to herd some of the sheep and goats back closer to the ger, so we manoeuvre our camels behind them to try to get them moving in the right direction. Surprisingly, this works, although we have the impression that the animals only take notice of what the local professional tells them to do and that the rest of us are just milling about uselessly.

I am pretty sure my camel has no respect for me at all and is only obeying those commands that seem likely to get him home as quickly as possible. Everything else he ignores. Oh, and a tip for any thrill-seeking camel jockeys reading this. If you are riding a camel and get a little bored with the slow pace, hold on tight before you kick your ride into second gear because when they start running it's like being on the back of a bucking bronco. Every part of the camel seems to have independent suspension. Your saddle has no suspension at all.

So, having learned our lesson, we all move at a sedate pace, swaying gently in the saddle, listening to the pitter-patter of the sheep and goats' hooves on the stony desert. Close your eyes and it sounds like raindrops. The camels are docile but moody. They are controlled, (if they want to be), via a rein attached to a piece of wood drilled through their nasal bone. A couple of them have collapsed humps and the boy explains that they are born that way. The family has forty camels but lost fifteen last year to wolves coming down from the mountains, which is why the remainder are now tethered close to the family gers. They do not use the camels as beasts of burden so much, now that they own a van, a trailer and a tractor for the annual move between summer and winter pasture, but they do use them for milk and sell their fur to traders from Ulaanbaatar.

As we return we see that all the baby goats, fifty or sixty of them, have been separated from the others and are grazing contentedly close to the gers. Our arrival in camp makes them scatter in a cacophony of high-pitched bleating. The remainder of the herd is scattered about the desert and we notice the lady of the house monitoring them from time to time from her front door, assisted by a pair of high-powered binoculars.

In the afternoon, when the sun is still beating down on us, we hike south west from the encampment where, we have been told, a river runs by. This seems unlikely given the hundreds of kilometres of dusty, dry landscape that we have passed through over the past couple of days, so we march out across the plain more in hope than expectation.

What a surprise it is then to crest a small ridge and find the plain drop away abruptly beneath us into a verdant canyon with a small stream trickling in the depths. A pasture of bright green grass covers much of the gully floor between sheer walls twenty to forty metres apart, suggesting that when it is not the dry season, a substantial river does indeed flow here. We are later told that the name of this river is Khongoryn Gol and it is the major water source for animals and humans alike in this part of the southern Gobi. Now, in the middle of dry season, sand-dunes tumble down the canyon walls in places right to the edge of the stream, where they form a muddy bank.

As we follow the stream around twists and turns in the gully, we come upon a herd of wild horses, led by a black stallion. They are feeding on the grass, drinking from the stream and wallowing in swampy mud-holes. The horses retreat from us at first but we climb a dune to take ourselves out of their threat zone and they turn back and continue on their way. The stallion always positions himself courageously between us and his herd as we follow, taking pictures. The horses lazily criss-cross the stream, but sun is setting, shadows are becoming longer and as the colours of the Gobi deepen, the green of the canyon floor contrasts gloriously with the reds and browns of the dunes and the canyon edge.

Back at camp later, we are entertained by the family's 700-strong herd of goats that are now hanging around waiting to be penned in for the night. They charge into and rub along the felt-covered ger walls and crowd around the entrance to peer in and see what we are doing. The babies are fun to watch as they play-butt each other and bounce around erratically as if electrocuted.

Our hosts join us for dinner, which includes borts, sticks of dried meat with the colour and consistency of wood. The Mongolians consume them with relish. Our pathetic weak teeth and jaws cannot handle them. We leave them mostly uneaten and this is regarded with astonishment. We explain that we are not hungry. We have noticed that all Mongolians young or old, have outrageously good teeth, white, strong and even. The same was true with the Buryatian people we met in Ulan Ude. It must be the diet. Western dentists should commission a study.

Our host has a television plugged in that is playing only static. He points it out proudly but complains that he has never managed to get it to work. Earlier we were watching his baby goats outside, using the satellite dish as a trampoline. We think we might have identified the problem and suggest he moves it to a goat-free location. He nods gratefully and offers us more borts.

The main piece of furniture in the ger is a sideboard topped with a series of faded pictures commemorating a trip to Ulaanbaatar many years before. We are reminded of something author John Man wrote. He observed that, with the demise of organised religion in rural Mongolia, family photographs today "take the place of household gods in rural gers."

As the sun drops over the horizon in the Gobi, the temperature plummets with it and after dinner we stand outside in the freezing night under a clear sky glistening with stars. The ger where we will sleep is a ghostly patch of dim light amid the darkness of the desert around us.

Bayanzag

Where we get some chores done, despair at our companions and find dinosaur eggs on flaming cliffs.

In the morning, we bid farewell to our hosts and leave early to start the drive north to the "flaming cliffs" of Bayanzag, one of the world's foremost sites for dinosaur remains. As soon as we leave camp the landscape starts to change, first to fields of yellow flowers then back to scrubby green pasture, before we are suddenly at the edge of the mountain range that has been our northern horizon for the last two days. We plunge into canyons between sheer rock walls that tower over us on both sides and hamsters fly from under our wheels as we bounce, shake and sway along the track.

Beyond the mountains we find ourselves back on the apparently endless plain but, after an hour or so, the tedium of the view is broken by the sight of a small town where we buy some basic food supplies, fix the exhaust on the van, top up our jerry cans with water from a mains pipe that a farmer has tapped to irrigate his field and idle away a couple of hours watching children playing in the streets.

The town is small, well-ordered, clean and tidy. Everyone is well-dressed and there is a substantial school near the main square. A few of the children are entertaining themselves, and us, exploding plastic bottles by stamping on them and sending the tops flying across the road. Others are kicking a football around. They are children from the Mongolian Gobi but they could be children anywhere in the world, apart from the fact that one of the girls, who looks about 6, is wearing battle fatigues and the boys actually take their shoes OFF to play football. They breed them tough out here.

Our translator and his pal the cook, just out of their teens themselves, cannot resist joining in the games, except that their concept of joining in is more akin to hijacking. They steal a little girl's bottle and start jumping on it themselves but are frustrated by their inability to make the top fly more than a couple of metres and give up. Then they borrow the ball and start kicking it to each other while the children just stand by, as bemused by their behaviour as we are.

Later in the day, when we stop at the tapped pipe to replenish our water supplies, our two heroes demonstrate again how much they have to learn about rural ways. They find it very difficult to fill the jerry cans, until the driver points out the top half of a plastic bottle that some kind soul has left there for passers-by to use as a funnel. This makes their job much easier and they are so impressed with this useful new tool that they pocket it and stow it in the van. Luckily, the driver spots what they have done before we drive away and makes them put it back.

We have noted on a number of occasions how clueless our translator and cook are about the world outside their home city. Although they are technically guides, they often act more like oblivious, starry-eyed tourists in a world not much less alien to them than it is to us. With the increasing number of Mongolians already living in Ulaanbaatar (home to 50% of the country's population of 2 million) and new urban centres planned for each province, the rural ways must be at risk of dying out, leaving only a pastiche to entertain tourists. When, later, we are all gathered together at dinner, I raise the issue and suggest that the survival of Mongolia's nomadic culture is under threat. Our driver agrees, shaking his head sadly.

Sofie and I wander off and pass a ramshackle hut with a cross on the roof. We peer in but there is no-one around apart from a couple of children who peer back at us through the fence and say "goodbye". Our two young companions claim Christianity as their religion and have suggested in conversation that their recent conversion to the faith is connected with the Korean Americans who have been teaching them English. It sounds like undercover missionaries are at work in the country.

At a house where our driver borrows a spot-welder to fix the exhaust, we are sitting outside on the street waiting for him to finish, when a large morose-looking dog mooches by with bits of blue and yellow rag tied around him. All over the countryside but especially by rivers and on mountain tops there are sacred mounds of stones called ovoos, which are characterised by the blue and yellow rags fluttering from them. This poor dog must have sat still for too long and been picked on by children to practice their ovoo-rag-tying skills.

Chores done, we head out of town across a flat green plain. After about half an hour, the earth suddenly falls away in front of us, the driver screeches to a halt in a cloud of dust and we find ourselves right on the edge of a gorge of rusty red sandstone cliffs falling away to where the plain continues over a hundred metres below.

This is Bayanzag. Some ancient seismic event must have raised the plain up along this fault and erosion over the centuries has forged the cliff line into its present form. The fresh rockslides visible along the cliff-line suggest that the process is continuing.

This is where Chapman Andrews in the 1920s and more recent expeditions have found dinosaur remains in almost unequalled abundance and species diversity.

Dinosaur finds apart, it is a spectacular view and we eagerly await the evening when the setting sun is supposed to turn the cliff-line fiery red. And that is exactly what happens. We walk along to the western-most promontory in the late afternoon and look back to see the sandstone scarlet and ablaze, a stark contrast with the green of the plain and the clear blue sky.

We clamber around the cliffs, spotting fossilised dinosaur eggs and searching hidden crevices in the rock for bones until the sun sets and we return to the top to set up camp. We do a little reconnaissance in the van, inspecting what look like potential shelters from the tireless but tiresome wind but, as usual, we find nowhere to hide.

It is not as fierce as the night we camped at Yolyn Am but it whines, whistles, surges and gusts; as invisible as ever. Only when it starts to swirl, picks up volumes of dust and sand and moves swiftly across the canyon floor do you see it. On a couple of occasions, as we were walking along the Bayanzag ridge, it tried to knock us over. Fortunately both times we saw the sandstorm build and race towards us, giving us time to crouch and curl up together beneath our hoodies before it hit us. It still spun us around and left us crunching and spitting sand for a while after it had moved on.

Ongiin Khiid

Where we visit the goat-infested rubble of a ruined monastery and finally have a shower!

Day dawns over the wind-swept plain and after a breakfast of sand-filled grits, we pack up once again, wrestling with the sand-filled debris of our tent and piling everything into the sand-filled interior of the van. Sofie announces that she "has had it with the desert." Her timing is perfect, as today we head north, back to the pastures of Central Mongolia. We stop briefly near a closed tourist ger camp to look at a small forest of saxaul shrubs, with their contorted trunks that dig deep beneath the sand to find the water table. Saxaul takes 25 years to reach maturity and a height of around four metres. It is a very hard wood; it burns like coal and is protected by law.

Our route north takes us through the middle of a patch of small dunes where sandstorms have obliterated all tracks and our driver must be operating from instinct or some internal compass. We finally reach the small town of Mandalovoo, where the wind is blowing dust and vegetation down the main street in a scene reminiscent of a classic cowboy movie. This is another quaint, clean, little desert town. There is some construction going on and in the town square we see our first cop of the week. You can tell he is a cop because he has the word Police (in English) on his tee shirt and on the back of his jeep.

Our crew commandeers an empty, abandoned restaurant to make us a special Mongolian lunch of "tsuivan" or fried noodles. In Mandalovoo we find the first toilet facility we have seen for five days, two small boxes built over a cesspit in the corner of a children's playground. There is one box for men and one for women and they measure about one metre tall by half a metre wide. You enter by first crouching then shuffling backwards looking through your legs so you can position your feet squarely on the two planks placed above the fetid pit below. Once inside you pull the door to, in order to shield yourself from the gaze of the crowd of children who have left the playground to watch this new entertainment.

Then, like Houdini in his magic box, you contort yourself and your clothing into the necessary posture to do what you have to do, sweat pouring down your face, as it is the middle of the day and the boxes are un-shaded. When you finally emerge and uncoil yourself in the fresh sweet-tasting air of the outside world you half-expect the attendant audience to erupt in a burst of applause. But the children just stare impassively, disappointed perhaps that you have not provided them with more drama.

At least it is a toilet. Normally in the Gobi, you just try to find somewhere secluded, which can be tricky on the flat featureless plain. There is often nowhere to hide. You can walk for miles and not come across even the smallest dip or gully. We find sarongs useful for preserving some privacy, although you can imagine what the wind does to the sarongs at the worst possible moment. You make your decision, check the wind direction as best you can, position yourself accordingly, then squat. When you have finished, you kick sand over the traces and just walk away, hoping that you never tread in someone else's camouflaged traces.

After lunch, another two hours in the van brings us to the ruins of the monastery of Ongiin Khiid. We wander around the piles of goat-infested rubble trying to visualise how the monastery must have looked in its prime, but it is difficult. The site is enormous and two determined campaigns of destruction, first by the Manchus then by the Soviet-inspired Mongolian KGB, to wipe both the monastery and the religion it represents from the face of the earth, have levelled it beyond all recognition. There is a memorial to the lamas slaughtered here by the KGB in the form of a list of names carved into a stone block. Apart from that, the only structures are a lone ger with three prayer wheels outside and a couple of new metal-roofed brick buildings that are locked.

We spot a group of local herdsmen, who approach one of the brick buildings and mill around outside for a couple of minutes until a woman appears with a key. When she opens the door we catch the scent of incense on the desert air. It is a small temple and we follow the herdsmen inside, trying to be as unobtrusive as possible. It is hardly a place for silent contemplation, though. The tin roof is loose and bangs and crashes violently in the wind.

The woman with the key gestures that we should follow her and leads us to the second brick building which seems to be something of a museum. It houses a variety of bric-a-brac in dusty glass cases, one of which contains a drinking vessel made from what appears to be a human skull. Nothing is labelled in any language so, after a quick look-around, we leave, none the wiser as to the point of it all. Maybe it is another Museum of Atheism?

Next to Ongiin Khiid is a huge tourist camp with a grey concrete wall around it, a massive stone statue of a goat and a monster banner bearing the legend Secret Mongolian History. We think this refers obliquely to "The Secret History of the Mongols", the story of Genghis Khan's life, dictated either by the great man himself or by someone very close to him, and Mongolia's most important contribution to world literature.

Our home for the night is in another, smaller, tourist ger camp just across the valley from the monastery. It is barely open and we are the only guests, but they have a bath-house with hot showers and, luxury of luxuries, a toilet you can sit on. Even better, we have a ger to ourselves and the beds have mattresses. However, this being Mongolia, although our ger is our own it is far from private. There is a small bolt on the door and we put it across while we change out of our desert clothes, but our translator rips it off when he barges in to see if we are happy with the accommodation. We point out the bolt now hanging off the door but he just laughs in delight. How silly we strange Westerners are, thinking that a small strip of metal like that can keep him out.

Challenged, that night we rig up a complex rope and pulley system attached to the roof structure of the ger and this works just fine in the morning when he tries to burst in and wake us up. He shakes the door until the whole ger is quivering but he cannot get in and has to be content with calling to us from outside. We revel in our small victory.

The Road to Khujirt

Where it is election day, we find ourselves back in green pastures and make some unannounced visits.

Today is Presidential Election Day in Mongolia and, when we leave our overnight base, we have a couple of passengers with us in the van; two girls from the ger camp who are going into the nearest town of Saikhan-Ovoo to vote. They tell us more about the ger camp. It has space for a hundred people in thirty gers, only three of which are set up at the moment. We are the first guests of the year. We think about the tiny bathhouse and reflect on our good fortune to have visited now, instead of in mid-summer at the height of the tourist season.

In town all the activity is centred on a two-storey brick building with the brightly coloured Mongolian flag flying high above it. No canvassing is permitted on Election Day itself, so the atmosphere outside in the main square is calm. The voters have come into town dressed in their smartest clothes, mostly brightly coloured robes with yellow or orange sashes tied around the middle, although some have chosen to wear a western-style suit, as shiny as possible of course, in imitation of the latest Russian fashions.

Naturally, everybody wears a hat. Headgear is a big deal in rural Mongolia. Trilbies, flat caps and baseball caps seem to be the preferred styles, and the manner of wearing your chosen headgear is dictated by the occasion. Our driver keeps his flat cap perched on his head at all times. It is usually at a jaunty angle when he is driving or relaxing but he straightens it up formally before entering a stranger's ger or stopping to talk to someone at the roadside.

We park outside what seems to be a local café with a secret entrance in the form of a hinged plank in the fence, although there don't seem to be any other entrances. Maybe it's a secret café. We wander over to the election hall. Inside there is the whispered formality of important events. Voters enter, remove their hats and show their ID to an official, who then finds their name in the electoral register and gives them a piece of paper. They carry this over to one of two desks positioned in each of the far corners of the hall. Each desk is isolated from the rest of the activity in the room and has a small three-sided raised metal structure on top so that voters can conceal their selection from prying eyes.

Having made their choice, they fold the piece of paper and place it in a large locked box in the centre of the hall, far away from the officials seated at their desks around the walls but in full sight of all. Before exiting, the voters have their identity checked again. Everything takes place in the presence of one official government observer and a member of each of the parties fielding a Presidential candidate, the Democratic Party and the Revolutionary Party, (which is the former Communist Party.)

Back in the van and back on the road, our translator makes a serious dent in his nation's musical reputation by singing verses from the two songs, "I Believe I Can Fly" and "Country Roads" over and over again, completely out of tune and randomly interchanging lines from both songs, all to the backing track of one of the driver's favourite Mongolian cassettes. The translator seems to have no self-consciousness at all but we cannot accuse him of not being great company, in his own eccentric way.

Today's lunch is going to be steamed dumplings, with goat meat again no doubt, and we pull up outside a solitary ger in the middle of the vast plain. The ger is surrounded by the usual expanse of animal droppings and assorted rusty metal objects such as a solar panel, a satellite dish, three motorbikes, some milk churns and a couple of trailers. Our crew calls out the customary greeting of "Hold Your Dog!" and the lady of the house comes to the door. After a further exchange, the boys follow her into the ger. At first, our driver stays in the van with us but, when he sees the man of the house heading over, he jumps out and engages him in conversation before they both go into the ger too. When they all emerge it transpires that they have negotiated an exchange, use of the family's cooking facilities against a share of our dumplings.

We follow them back inside, adopting the customary entry procedure. You step over, (never on) the threshold. The woman of the house is always the one who greets you outside and follows you in. The man of the house waits inside on his bed facing the door.

To our western eyes, the invasion of a family's privacy by complete strangers is distasteful and we ask later if such customs extend to the city. For example, would similar hospitality be extended to someone who just turned up unannounced at the door of the translator's family's flat in Ulaanbaatar and asked to use the kitchen. He confesses that someone who tried to do this would be viewed suspiciously and would be unlikely to be allowed past the flat's bolted steel grill. He explains that rural hospitality to travellers is a tradition dating back many centuries and that, up to as little as five years ago, countryside-dwellers who were away from home during the day would leave their doors unlocked and a cooked meal ready on the table just in case any hungry travellers passed by while they were out. We ask why this is no longer practiced and he replies that, with the growth of tourism in Mongolia, the open generosity of the country folk has been abused on occasions. Word has got around and people now lock their doors when they leave home.

On the positive side though, he adds, some of the more entrepreneurial families, such as the one we stayed with in the southern Gobi, have taken to putting up extra gers to accommodate visitors and charging people to stay the night as well as organising camel rides and other excursions. There is a company called "Ger to Ger" which even arranges for tourists to accompany nomadic families on their annual migration and help with the housework and herding. Westerners pay a healthy sum for the experience. The Mongolians must find it incredible that people will pay the equivalent of six months income for a week of sleeping on the ground, milking yaks and chasing goats for a week. It is unlikely that those Mongolians who have escaped the rural yoke for the bright lights of Ulaanbaatar harbour much nostalgia for the hard ways of the past.

Our misgivings over disturbing the locals disappear as soon as we are all seated around the table in the ger. The family is genuinely pleased to hear news from beyond the horizon and conversation flows easily. Our team makes buuz, (steamed dumplings), for them and they make tea and dried goat meat with noodles for us. The tea is made with goat's milk and salt and is served accompanied by rock-hard biscuits and a very sour, cheesy, curd. While cooking, our guys go out of their way to be as unobtrusive as possible and clean up after themselves impeccably.

Our driver is the ultimate diplomat and has a gift for putting people at their ease. He is especially comfortable bonding with the men of the house, who talk a lot but actually, as we have seen, do very little except when it comes to manly tasks like killing wolves. The Mongolian women shoulder alone the burden of running the household and the animals. As our translator puts it, the main function of Mongolian men is to "hang out with their peers."

As we are leaving, we observe an interesting technological variation on rural ways when the son of the house turns up herding two horses and a foal on his motorbike. He then switches to horseback to herd the goats and sheep. Later in the day, further along the road, we see another guy herding horses on a motorbike. Modern days require modern ways. We are in the grasslands now, back in the more typical Mongolian landscape of rolling tree-less green hills and big blue sky. This is horse country. We see hundreds of them and are struck by their variety. The Mongolians apparently have 300 words to distinguish horses by their coat colouring and pattern.

We pass a number of lakes, many of which are dry and distinguishable as lakes only by what look like salt deposits on the cracked brown earth. This is the dry season, after all. But there is still water in some lakes and we even see small streams flowing between the hills in places. The Gobi is definitely behind us now, although we still see the odd dust storm swirl up in the distance and we are still creating quite a trail ourselves as we charge along.

The animal life has changed too. We now see cranes swooping over the meadows and hawks and eagles hovering up high. One bird of prey sitting on a rock by the side of the track eyes us coldly as we flash by. We start to see our first yaks of the trip, big hairy cows. We read so much about them before coming here but have seen none on our journey so far. They are evidently not suited to the harsh Gobi climate. We stop for tea at another ger late in the afternoon but do not feel as welcome this time. The experience is mildly awkward, reminiscent of visiting distant relatives as a child. We sit in silence as our team labours to make stilted conversation and everyone rush-slurps the oily goats milk tea so we can get out of there as quickly as possible. Soon after, we cross one of Mongolia's few blacktop roads where there is a truck-stop café, our first glimpse of the new Mongolia for a week. Maybe in future, travellers will stop at places like this instead of the rural family gers?

In the evening we arrive in Khujirt, a town famed for its hot springs. We take a quick look around a Soviet-style green and white block that has been constructed over the springs. The building houses a hotel and sanatorium providing mud-bath treatments. We consider staying there but the room we are shown wins this month's prize for "Most Disgusting." Remarkably, the toilet smells worse than any we have encountered on this trip so far. There have been several worthy contenders but this one wins hands-down. Instead we choose to stay in a ger in the camp next door, which, heights of luxury, has both a stove and a power socket. We take the opportunity to charge cameras and phones to give our capable but slow mini-solar charger a break. Then we get the stove going in order to ward off the cold of the evening. We settle down for the night but find it hard to sleep as we are constantly disturbed by sounds of civilisation outside: barking dogs, car horns beeping and people moving around. The ceaseless roar of the Gobi wind was much more soothing.

Karakorum

Where we look in vain for traces of Genghis Khan in his ancient capital, listen to Mongolian throat singing, ride Mongolian horses and eat yet more goat.

We continue our journey north towards the monasteries of Shankh Khiid and Erdene Zuu and the ancient capital of Karakorum. We are still very much in horse territory and pass several large herds grazing on the seemingly endless meadows. Here and there we see mounted horsemen. With their long coats obscuring most of their legs and, with the comparatively short stature of the Mongolian horses, they look like two parts of the same animal, half-man-half horse. No wonder ancient European maps depicted the people who lived to the east of the Altai mountains as mythical centaur-like four-legged beings.

The relative heights of Mongolian horse and man mean that a man mounted on a horse is not much taller than he would be if he were standing next to the horse. The other thing that contributes to the impression that horse and rider are one entity is the Mongolian riding style, which involves very little up-and-down movement. The rider stays completely still in the saddle. The only movement comes from the horse, which seems to scuttle and shuffle along rather than canter or gallop.

The first place we visit is the Shankh Khiid monastery, a small complex located all alone on a remote hillside, with a small collection of huts around the walls. We arrive as the resident monks – of all ages from 8 to 80 - are chanting in a small building to the side of the main temple. The room is fitted out with pews and desks. Incense fills our dry Gobi-ravaged nostrils as we observe silently from a corner, feeling very privileged to be there and witnessing their rituals. It is a beautiful day, the warmest of our trip so far, and I don't know if it is the serene calm of the monastery, the balmy weather, the incense, the chanting or a combination of all these things, but the world feels remarkably wonderful. We are thus in a great mood for Erdene Zuu, a short drive away. This is Mongolia's largest monastery and one that is apparently working hard to return to somewhere near its former glories after the damage wreaked during the Soviet era.

It helps that the level of destruction meted out to Erdene Zuu by the Mongolian KGB in 1937 was less all-devouring than to other monasteries, such as Onghiin Khid. A large number of old artefacts have survived, including some 17th century wall paintings that you would have expected to have been tempting targets for the thugs with axes and sledgehammers. There must be a reason for this but, although we ask, we don't learn anything.

A young local guide who speaks passable English accompanies us on our tour. Although reluctant to get drawn into politics and the history of the site, she is nevertheless a veritable font of knowledge on Buddhism, the monastery and the artworks on display. One of the temples within the 400-square-metre complex is a working building made of white bricks in the Tibetan style and here again we are fortunate to arrive while a group of thirty or so monks are sitting at prayer, their chants accompanied by the rhythmic clash of cymbals.

Karakorum, the ancient capital of Genghis Khan, no longer exists, as the Manchus of the Qing Dynasty destroyed it and its stones were quarried to build the vast walls of Erdene Zuu. The town today is part hillside village, part industrial complex. With its blacktop roads and hustle and bustle, Karakorum feels urban and modern compared to the countryside we have travelled through. A week ago it would probably have felt like the end of the world. We are still 360 kms away from Ulaanbaatar, so technically this is still rural Mongolia.

We move into a ger camp close to the monastery walls and have a lunch of goat milk and huustuu, large flat pancakes filled with diced goat. We eat to the accompaniment of furious bleating from herds of goats and sheep around the camp. They are no doubt celebrating the fact that they haven't made it into the pot yet. Their turn will come, that much is certain.

In the afternoon we walk into town past the monastery, a distance of three or four kilometres. We pass an ovoo and walk around it three times clockwise as you are supposed to, adding a further stone to the pile. We count exactly one hundred stupas in total on the monastery walls: a statistic that on its own gives you a good idea of the immense size of the place.

In town we come upon the central commercial district, which consists of shipping containers, (now shopping containers) set up in lines around two small squares. One of the squares is full of people playing pool on a dozen or so tables that have been set up in the open air. Even though it is late afternoon by now and a few of the containers have been locked up for the day, what seems to be the full spectrum of Karakorum society is milling about, including a number of men in full rural Mongolian garb of long coat with long sleeves and heavy knee high boots. They look very cool and show no signs of discomfort despite the blistering heat of the day.

We attract a lot of attention as the only non-Mongolians in sight and are approached by a girl in her early twenties who wants to practice her English. She, like our travelling companions, has been studying in a school run by Koreans. We find a mini-mart close to the bus station and stock up on supplies as well as gifts for our team members, whom we will be leaving tomorrow

Back at the camp an old man in ceremonial dress is giving a Mongolian music recital and invites us to come along and listen. He plays a variety of instruments and sings along, treating us to our first experience of Mongolian nose, tongue, throat and chest singing, all of which seem to involve sealing various bodily air chambers and causing them to vibrate independently. Sometimes he manages to get two chambers to vibrate simultaneously. He is an amateur but quite a virtuoso, at least to our untutored ear, and the concert lasts around 45 minutes. We decline the opportunity to buy a CD but leave a few thousand Togrog instead as a gesture of appreciation.

The following day begins with a trip up into the hills above Karakorum to see one of two giant stone turtles, the only artefacts of ancient Karakorum that have survived, although they evidently get moved around a bit. Pictures in the guide books show them in a variety of locations. Today, so we are told, at least one is on top of a hill overlooking the monastery and we hire a guide and some horses to go up and see it. The guide is late and, when he does eventually appear, greets us memorably by evacuating both nostrils forcibly in our direction before shaking hands. We flinch but are too late to move out of the way.

The horses are fitted with Mongolian saddles, which turn out to be very uncomfortable, especially if you are male and riding downhill. However, this is the most Mongolian of all forms of transport and therefore an appropriate way to explore the Mongolian countryside. The turtle is unimpressive, as is a nearby ovoo, ostentatiously and photogenically decorated with a line of animal skulls. However, the views of Karakorum and Erdene Zuu from the top of the hill are wonderful. Perhaps that is why they have moved the turtle up there.

The Mongolian horses are small and sturdy and mine seems to sense my inexperience. Sofie is a natural rider and has no difficulty at all. My horse makes it obvious that it bitterly resents having been removed from the herd to cater to a tourist who evidently has no idea what to do with a horse and it whinnies with passionate jealousy as we canter past a herd, unencumbered by passengers, quietly enjoying a light snack on the prairie. On our descent my horse decides it has had more than enough and tries to change course and go straight to its home ger to the south of the hills. It takes more than a little gentle persuasion and the intervention of the guide to persuade it to stick to the original plan. When we return our crew asks us what we think of the famous Mongolian horses. When we mention their diminutive size, this seems to cause offence so we quickly change the subject.

The guys have spent the morning preparing a typical Mongolian stone hotpot for us. This consists of half a goat, some root vegetables and a dozen smooth round stones picked up from the desert, all boiled in a potage of goat fat in a wok on a dung-filled stove. The first part of the eating ritual is to remove the burning hot stones from the goat fat with your fingers and juggle them from hand to hand. We are initially reluctant to get involved with this part of the process, mainly because, as it has been throughout the trip, our water supply for washing is limited and hot water is non-existent. But our hosts insist that it is an essential part of the ritual so we join in. We realise quickly that it is a bit of a dexterity test. It is important to shift the stones around fast to avoid getting blisters. Soon, as anticipated, our hands and wrists are covered in goat grease before we have even started eating.

We take a look in the pot now the stones have been removed and discarded and see a jawbone with teeth poking appetisingly out of the layer of bubbling animal fat. The smell of goat fills our ger and, indeed, it will be a couple of days and a few hot showers before we stop smelling of goat ourselves.

The hotpot is tasty but much of it is indigestible gristle, something you only ever discover after it is already in your mouth and you have started chewing. We struggle to keep up with our companions and share their obvious delight in this special meal. The decibel level of the lip-smacking, slurping and sighing is even higher than normal. However, we realise that we have more than met our match, not for the first time around a dining table in Mongolia, when one of the boys snaps a bone in two and uses the pointed end of another bone to extract the marrow and fork it into his mouth. He suggests we follow his lead and do the same. We decline.

Ulaanbaatar

Where we experience both summer and winter in one day and unexpectedly find that we quite like Mongolia's quirky capital city

After lunch, we leave Karakorum for the long trek back to Ulaanbaatar. At first we eat up the distance on a blacktop road but this runs out after about 200 kilometres, just beyond the Tuul River and near the town of Luun, where we stop for a break. Still full of goat hot pot we decide not to join our crew for an afternoon snack of goat noodles and instead go for a stroll along the river. We stop by a small lake and are casually watching a herd of horses rolling around in a dust patch just beyond the lake when we notice one horse which has hung back near the river, away from the rest of the herd, and seems distressed. We can see what seems to be another horse's head poking up over the riverbank and go over to investigate.

As we approach, the distressed horse runs off to join the rest of the herd and, when we arrive at the riverbank, we find two horses that have managed to get themselves tied up in a length of rope. Neither can move independently and we can see open wounds on both horses caused by the chafing of the rope as they struggle to free themselves. We are tempted to intervene but are wary of how the horses will react and then we notice a man leading another horse away from the river a few hundred metres away.

We run over to him and try to explain what we have found. English doesn't work. Chinese doesn't work and we have no Mongolian so we try Russian and this time we manage to get the message across. "Ya znaio!, (I know!)" he says curtly.

We head slowly back towards the van looking over our shoulder now and again to see if anything is being done about the tangled-up horses. After a few minutes we see a motorbike speeding towards the river with two people on board. They disappear down the bank and a moment later we see the two horses appear trotting along happily, apparently none the worse for their ordeal.

The journey to Ulaanbaatar seems to take forever. Once the tarmac runs out, the pot-holed dirt road is far worse than any of the Gobi tracks we have experienced and, close as we are to the capital, gives a terrible impression of the country's infrastructure.

When we finally arrive, it is a warm evening and the city has the air of a Southeast Asian metropolis. We could be in Manila, Jakarta, Bangkok or Kuala Lumpur. Street sellers line neon-lit pavements washed with music pouring out of shops and restaurants and patrolled by westernised teenagers. Groups of boys in faux hip-hop gear manufacture a swagger, while girls in string tops and short shorts sway along arm in arm and giggle loudly to confuse the boys.

Couples sit long over their drinks outside street-side cafes and the line of pizzerias and burger joints is interspersed with local food outlets. This is fashionable west-central "UB" and we are in a guest house just off the main road, opposite the flash State Department Store 1921-2009, a relic of the Soviet era but now home to outlet stores selling famous brands to an affluent clientele.

In the morning, the city is transformed. Gone is the colourful, bustling Asian capital simmering on a warm spring night. It has been replaced by an ugly, grey Soviet-Siberian city freezing in near zero temperatures under a sky the colour of your grandmother's old over-washed underwear. We walk towards the city-centre hoping for some respite from the ubiquitous ugliness but only find a series of bright orange-pink statues adorning squares surrounded by what look like Russian mausoleums.

Traffic roars noisily and moves at random, ignoring traffic lights, bored cops and pedestrian crossings. We are almost run over twice by what looks like the same banana-yellow Hyundai Accent. We think we are being targeted by a psychopath until we realise that there are hundreds of these cars around and they are all the same colour. They are the only bright spots on the drab grey of the streets, apart from the pink statues, of course. We are happy that we only have twenty-four hours here: just enough time to check emails, pick up our onward train tickets, get some laundry done and do a little food shopping. Prices in shops and restaurants seem to be ten times what they were out in the countryside but at least we can finally eat something other than goat.

In the afternoon, the snow that has threatened all day starts to fall in the world's coldest capital. We have gone from summer to winter and experienced a temperature drop of more than thirty degrees. We walk to the outdoor train museum to take some pictures for a friend who is a railway fanatic and notice a thick covering of snow on the mountains that encircle the city. On the way back we stop at a coffee bar, which manages to improve our impression of Ulaanbaatar considerably. The bar is a little oasis of warmth and cosiness; beautifully decorated and lit, with a large aquarium and a luxurious VIP room at the back. The waitresses are attentive and efficient.

Another incident that serves to raise the city's star still further in our eyes takes place shortly afterwards, when we are looking for an English language bookshop mentioned in the guidebook. The street number given turns out to be a pharmacy. We walk in, realise our mistake and immediately turn to leave. But, as we do so, one of the pharmacy staff rushes out and, guessing what we are searching for, directs us to the bookshop, which is two doors down the block. We thank her and she says "bye-bye" with a wave and a big smile. These are small things but make a world of difference to how a visitor feels about a place. We think they resonate even more strongly with us because they contrast so starkly with the cold indifference we received as strangers in shops and restaurants in Russia.

On the Trans-Mongolian

Where we get our health checked and our wheels changed on our way into China.

In order to get to China, we need to cross the Gobi again, this time by Trans-Mongolian train. In Mongolia, there is a barbed wire fence running along both sides of the track, no doubt to stop sheep, goats, cows, horses or camels from resting, grazing or dying on the rails. As we have seen on countless occasions over the past week, the fact that animals are used to roaming wherever they want presents a major problem for Mongolian drivers. Loud blasts on the horn usually manage to shift them, but sheep in particular tend to respond to being startled by running straight towards the car and playing a game of "chicken", (or should it be "mutton") that they cannot win. You can imagine the carnage that would ensue if the train tracks were not fenced in.

This section of the Gobi is featureless but occasionally there is a little light entertainment when we hit a patch of low sand dunes on the line and churn up an impressive sandstorm for a few kilometres. From time to time we spot a lone orange-jacketed figure standing by the track with a flag raised, waving the train through. This is the same pose we have seen adopted by European and Russian stationmasters throughout this trip. However, here there are no stations and no platforms. There are not even any villages in sight, just sand and stones. Who knows how far they have had to come just to stand there at a set time each day to give the all clear as we trundle by? And how do they know it IS all clear?

At the tiny village of Zamiin Uud going out through Mongolian border control is much less entertaining than coming in. There are no smugglers this time and I am not hauled off the train for a midnight interview in the immigration office. Strangely, the officials here all seem to be female and are incongruously glamorous in their high heels and short skirts. Even the troops guarding the train to make sure we don't jump off are female and look like catwalk models just pretending to be soldiers.

We only stop for an hour before the train comes to life again and shudders off across no-mans-land into China. Suddenly there are billboards in Chinese characters and we find ourselves in Erlyan, which looks like a big city. After we pull into the station, officials again board the train, there are a few forms to fill in and, in a new development, everyone has their temperature taken by a thermometer thrust into the armpit.

The health check is evidently taken seriously. (Having had no news for weeks, when I wrote these lines we were completely unaware of the H1N1 swine flu pandemic that was sweeping the world at the time.) There is also an official on the platform who looks like an astronaut in his shiny white full body environmental protection suit. He is carrying an equally shiny, bright-white box – the sort of thing the guys who took ET away were equipped with. During the whole process, there is French Can-Can music playing over the station sound system, which only serves to enhance the otherworldly feel of it all.

Then we face a long, long wait while the wheels on the carriages are changed to conform to Chinese track size. All the passengers stay on the train while this is going on. We are towed to a long railway shed where the carriages are separated and then raised up on hydraulic lifts so that the Russian bogies can be removed and replaced by Chinese bogies. There is lots of jostling and jolting and everything is done by hand with workers crawling around under the cars while the passengers peer out of the almost opaque, sand-blasted windows, cameras in hand. If there are model train nerds among them, they must be consumed with envy watching these guys playing with real toys.

Eventually we have new wheels and our passports are returned. We climb into bed and are asleep before the train pulls out. We sleep soundly. Our new Chinese wheels feel a lot smoother than our old Russian/Mongolian wheels.

When we wake, we are beyond Datong, 300 kilometres from Beijing and travelling through paddy fields with a range of mountains to our left and another, more distant, to our right. The sun is shining on the people bent over working in the fields and glinting off their bicycles parked nearby. We see donkeys and bullocks pulling ploughs, rows of small houses with red-tiled roofs and occasionally an orchard enclosed by mud-brick walls.

This pastoral scene is very different from the Gobi landscape that we travelled through yesterday. The countryside has a very Mediterranean feel to it, an impression enhanced by the sight of avenues of cypress and poplars, their leaves flashing silver as they catch the sunlight. Although it is fertile and green, you can see that the trees are rooted in sandy soil . The dusty, dry terrain that has accompanied us throughout all the thousands of kilometres we have covered since Warsaw is still with us. As the valley narrows and the mountains to the right come closer to the tracks, we see rice terraces cut into the foothills and a village with a ten-metre-high mud wall surrounding it.

This train is packed full of European tourists and we wonder where they have all come from. All the way across Russia and Siberia as far as Irkutsk we saw only Russians on the trains. Certainly in the Altai we were the only foreigners, at least as far as we could tell. We saw a couple of French guys and a small group of elderly Japanese tourists in Listvyanka but it was not until we were on the Ulan Ude to Ulaanbaatar train that we spotted the first signs of the designer Berghaus brigade.

Now, heading for Beijing, the corridors resonate with conversations in Dutch and French, and high-powered, high-priced video cameras are being pointed at the dusty carriage windows and the horizon beyond. We debate amongst ourselves how it is that we have not encountered these folk before, with their loud voices, loud clothing and patient tour guides. Maybe the Trans-Siberian / Trans-Mongolian tourist season has caught up with us?

The houses in the hillside villages among the rice terraces are made from the same red earth as the hills themselves. They look ancient and timeless. The way the man-made structures blend into the natural landscape reminds us of French villages like Les Baux in Provence, where we practiced our tent-erecting and outdoor cooking skills before embarking on this trip.

We are in Hebei Province now, close to Zhangjiakou. There is lots of water in the rice paddies but none in the sandy, dried up, river beds which we cross. A muddy creek tries to dribble on alongside us as we rattle down the track but gives up after a short while.

As we pull into Zhangjiakou, a small town (in Chinese terms) of around a million inhabitants, we see hundreds of men on the lines beside us, all dressed in identical bright yellow hard-hats. Some wave at the train, others sit on the tracks staring at us impassively. None is actually doing anything.

We eventually come upon the mountains and pass through them via a dozen tunnels, maybe more. The mountains tower above us. Sometimes they are just bare rock, sometimes they are covered completely in trees and shrubs. We are now following a river with fast-flowing water. The trees are bent over it, suggesting that the wind is blowing a gale, despite the clear blue skies. We hope we are arriving in Beijing after the annual sandstorm season. This would be excellent news. We have had enough of sand for the time being.

The river alongside us has become enormous. It is now several hundred metres across and is pouring through a wide picturesque mountain gorge. There are a dozen orange-helmeted people in a rubber jet boat shooting downstream. Fishermen line the riverbank with makeshift shades set up against the sun, couples stroll through the woods and families hold picnics in clearings amid the trees. It is Friday morning but it looks like a weekend. We see a jetty with some large boats tied up next to it then a huge dam appears and suddenly, that's it, no more river, just a little stream trickling along.

Images

Diorama of Mongol siege of Vladimir, 1238.

Wooden Palace, Suzdal

Platform teddy bear seller doing great business.

Our Altai base camp

Lake Teletskoye

Giant Lenin's Head, Ulan Ude

Ulan Ude Station, early morning

Fuelling our trusty ride, Gobi Desert

Camel team heading for the dunes

Camping on Mars

Writing on Mars

Erdene Zuu, Karakorum

Musician, Karakorum Ger Camp

Heading back across the Gobi by train

Changing our wheels

Hostel in the Beijing Hutongs

Pingyao Main Street

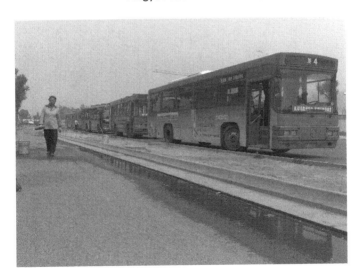

Bus no. 4, Xian

Terracotta warriors, Bingmayong, Xian

Bronze horses, Bingmayong, Xian

Our route through Europe. A. Ghent, B. Cologne, C. Warsaw, D. Vilnius, E. Riga, F. Moscow, G. Vladimir / Suzdal

Our route through Asia. H. Novosibirsk, J. Altai Mountains, K. Irkutsk, L. Ulan Ude, M. Ulaanbaatar, N. South Gobi, O. Beijing, P. Pingyao, Q. Xian, R. Guilin

§3

China

Beijing: Heavenly Peace, Heavenly Temple

Where we hit the streets, see the sights and accidentally find ourselves in a hospital, although there is no accident.

We enter Beijing, a city the size of Belgium with twice the population, almost an hour before our scheduled arrival time and rattle through mile after mile of suburbs. These consist mainly of tall, Hong Kong-style apartment blocks, mostly new, clean and bright, with large windows. They are a world away from the grey Soviet hulks that have blighted the outskirts of every city we have seen since we entered Russia. We pass through the ultra-modern railway station of Beijing South, with its platforms lined with sleek, white, space-shuttle-like trains, and feel a little old-fashioned in our dusty old diesel.

At Beijing Central the train empties with astonishing speed and we manoeuvre our way through the throngs up to the main concourse. Three great things about international train travel compared to air travel are, a) you carry your baggage with you; b) you go through immigration formalities on the train, and c) when you arrive, you are already in the city centre. There is no queue, no officialdom, no pointless hanging around and no need to take a shuttle anywhere.

We emerge from the concourse into a 21st century city basking under blue skies. Wide thoroughfares are flanked by flashy skyscrapers of glass and steel. Large banks of flower beds are being hosed down by a small army of gardeners, who flash gold-toothed smiles as we pass by. Fashionable city-folk stroll along, many with parasols to prevent their skin from becoming darkened by the summer sun that beats down on the streets.

It is all very reminiscent of Hong Kong until you look a little closer. Here and there, pavement stones are missing, leaving gaping holes. On every corner there are police or Public Security Bureau watchers, some in uniform, others in civilian clothes but wearing red and yellow armbands to distinguish them.

We turn into the pedestrianised shopping avenue of Wangfujing, where massive screens blare out announcements and advertising and where a parade of big retail names have set up shop. Armani has an entire building, sandwiched in the middle of a strip of Chinese pharmacies and local fashion outlets. In the centre of the street is a mini fairground with a catapult, a virtual space-ship ride and drinks stalls selling a mixture of Western and Chinese concoctions, staffed by keen young Beijngers in a variety of McDonalds-style uniforms. We follow our map through the side streets to the west of Wangfujing and a final turn next to a brand new police headquarters brings us to the Jade International Hostel. With its marble lobby and comfortable rooms, it feels like a three star hotel rather than the backpacker joint that it is. The location is as perfect as we had hoped. From our window on the 8th floor we can see the roofs of the Forbidden City below.

When we go out in the evening to explore, our first stop is the Foreign Languages Bookstore back on Wangfujing as we need a Chinese dictionary as well as some more reading material. We have given away all the books we departed with to people we met along the way. We then head for Tiananmen Square, pausing briefly en route to eat a bowl or two of jiaozi (dumplings) in a small street-side restaurant. Instead of following the traffic, we turn into a narrow park where willow trees drape themselves around colourful bridges laid across a small canal. People from the nearby hutongs sit out in the pagodas enjoying the warm evening, couples cuddle demurely on half-hidden benches by the water and the whole place exudes an air of calm tranquillity.

This is in striking contrast to what we find when we come out of the park and find ourselves amid the hubbub of Tiananmen Square. Ironically, we are right next to the Gate of Heavenly Peace where Mao gazes down benignly on a heaving throng of folk. These are mainly Chinese visitors, taking pictures of each other in front of the backdrop of the Great Helmsman or watching the line of spot-lit dancing fountains that have been set up beneath the southern wall of the Forbidden City.

As the sun has already set, the square itself is sealed off and the central obelisk and Mao's mausoleum (the Maosoleum?) sit alone and unattended in the middle of kilometres of white temporary crowd control fencing. It is June 1st, three days before the twentieth anniversary of the storming of the Square to clear the students, a day which probably feels like yesterday to the Party leaders. On a connected issue the hotel TV has 70 channels but they are all Chinese; no BBC, no CNN, no Deutsche Welle. In Russia we could pick up the BBC, although there were still no American channels, not even in Moscow.

We leave the Square, once again taking a detour through the park and, still hungry, head for the night market on Donghuamen. This is a bit of a tourist trap with its fried silkworms, scorpion kebabs, sheep penises and dried starfish. But it is fun to see and you can eat well here, albeit not very cheaply. It is brash, noisy and intimidating at first but we dive in and end up with har gau (prawn dumplings), sweetcorn on sticks, rou jiaomo (meat sandwiches) and fried vegetable jiaozi before the raucous screeching of the vendors becomes too irritating and we escape to the calm of our hostel.

It is ten years since I was last in Beijing and although one or two elements, such as the night market, are familiar, the streets have changed almost beyond recognition, at least superficially. We are here less than a year after the Olympics, so we are benefitting from the results of the huge beautification programme the authorities put the city through in order to wow the world.

The next morning, one priority is to try to find dim sum, which is a passion of ours and something we have been looking forward to for weeks. We know that dim sum is a peculiarly Hong Kong phenomenon and that it is rare to encounter it in Beijing. Our guidebooks had no listings, nor could our hostel reception help. However, we have seen distinct Hong Kong influences in the template by which the skyscrapers of central Beijing and the apartments of the suburbs have been designed, and this gives us cause for optimism. The first place we look is in the Oriental Plaza, a plush mall that looks like it has been plucked from the streets of Kowloon. It is an inspired choice. We descend below street level and immediately find a restaurant with an excellent and authentic dim sum menu. We proceed to gorge ourselves on har gau, siu mai (pork and shrimp dumplings), char siu bau (roast pork buns) and the like.

Just as the Oriental Plaza would not look out of place in Tsimshatsui, nor would the shoppers thronging its designer stores. Adidas, Nike and Jordan are here, as are a number of Chinese fashion chains and specialist outlets. The people of downtown Beijing are very different from the ballcapped rural folk in the groups we saw touring Tiananmen Square last night. They are fashionable, urbane, sophisticated and, let's face it, rich.

Hundreds of people are gathered in the main atrium of the mall waiting for a celebrity singer to show up to do a Clairol promotion and there is a doll painting event going on elsewhere.

We decide to walk to the Temple of Heaven and, seeking out some shade, we leave the main streets and enter a small park. Strolling through, we notice that most of the people in the park are male, some are in pyjamas and many are working out gently on exercise machines. Then we notice a group of nurses and a couple of men in white coats and it dawns on us that we must have stumbled upon some sort of sanatorium. Sure enough, as we emerge from the park on the other side we find the main entrance of Beijing Hospital right in front of us. No wonder we were getting even more than our usual share of strange looks.

The gardens around the Temple of Heaven are quite simply beautiful. The signature structures are set in the middle of an enormous green lung filled with pine and cypress trees. Old men have brought their caged songbirds out and hang them in the trees while they sit below in silent contemplation. The bird song is our background music as we stroll. Approaching the Ming and Qing dynasty temples, the soundtrack to the afternoon changes and our exploration is accompanied by soft Chinese music emanating from discreetly located speakers.

As we wander through the park we are not alone but, far from being a source of irritation, the local tour groups provide great entertainment. Their guides manage to convince them to do the strangest things. At one point they queue up to stand on a stone and have their picture taken, even though the stone itself will not actually feature in any of the pictures, and they contort themselves into ever more bizarre and creative shapes as they pose, each one trying to outdo their predecessor.

Elsewhere they take it in turns to hold out their arms theatrically towards an ancient juniper tree, (to feel its aura, maybe?) More fun is provided by the hard-working army of plastic bottle collectors who patrol the park. Their activities are sanctioned to the extent that there are signs prohibiting visitors from picking up discarded bottles themselves. They can be a little over enthusiastic; we saw one poor guy having a water bottle torn from his grasp when it was still half-full.

The Temple of Heaven grounds are an oasis of peace away from the concrete and traffic of the city, although it has to be said that so far we have not yet experienced Beijing's infamous pollution. The traffic has been much lighter and the air much cleaner than we expected. The overall impression of this part of the city is one of space. The crowds and bustle that we are used to in Hong Kong are absent, even in the market streets of Qianmen, which our route takes us through on the way home from the temples.

Known in the past as the silk district, Qianmen seems to be an up-and-coming shopping area. A brand new precinct, modelled after a typical merchant's quarter in old China, has just been completed, with shops being fitted out and decorated, although, of the first tenants, only H & M has its doors open for business.

From Qianmen we cross the road via an underpass to Tiananmen Square, going through bag security but avoiding a random body search, although the guy after us got one. We pass the mausoleum and are just admiring the scene when the police start their evening clearance operation. Buses draw up in the middle of the square and hundreds of uniformed officers form a cordon that moves slowly outwards, herding the crowd before it back into the subways. Recorded announcements in Chinese and English declare that the Square is now closed and all visitors should leave. Only when the Square is completely clear and the subways sealed do they switch on the floodlights illuminating the monument in the centre. In addition to the uniformed police we notice a number of plain clothes officers working in the square, distinguished from the throng by their tight haircuts, tanned-faces and radio-bulges under their shirts.

Our last task of the day is to find a restaurant serving Peking duck and we pick a branch of Quanjude, located on the 4th floor of a shopping centre in Wangfujing. The restaurant is strangely hard to find in the evening as the escalators to the upper floors are shut down and blocked off early, hours before the restaurant closes. After searching for a few minutes, we find we need to go through to the back of the store and take the cargo lift up to the 4th floor. But the quest for Quanjude is well worth the effort: great Peking duck and great value.

Beijing: Hutongs

Where we explore the old lanes of central Beijing and come across a fortune-telling bird.

Day three in Beijing and we set off on another marathon walk through the city. We tramp along the wide boulevards, where the blistering heat is reflected and amplified by the shimmering steel and glass, then turn off the main street into the relative cool of the hutongs, to begin wandering randomly in this maze of narrow streets that surrounds the Forbidden City. The hutongs are mostly one-storey terraced dwellings built along lanes based on an east-west grid. They were established by the Mongols in the 13th century while they were rebuilding Beijing, (having first completely destroyed it, of course.)

Traditionally all front doors face south, like Mongolian gers, and the lanes are connected by north-south alleyways. The hutongs are home to thousands of Beijing city-folk, although fewer than before, as many of the hutongs were torn down to permit the construction of new roads and facilitate pre-Olympic beautification projects. The hutong network is nevertheless still extensive. It is a hive of activity and there is renovation / restoration work going on everywhere.

We pass one section full of tiny fashion stores and another busy area of bars and cafes, where well-dressed young Beijingers are enjoying a lazy afternoon grouped around tables or reclining on sofas in the shade. Some hutong hotels and bars have been adopted by the western backpacker community and in fact, you can find almost anything as you wander through the lanes, from massage services to skateboard outlets. The walls may be uniformly grey but many of the houses have multi-coloured gabled roofs and wood-panelled interiors.

Next to the Zhongzizhang metro station, we come upon what turns out to be an excellent pizzeria called The Park, (we still cannot get used to all the food options here, compared to those available in Mongolia.) The upper storey looks out into a courtyard of a building that used to be the headquarters of the Chinese Navy in Qing dynasty times. The staff are relaxing, (read "comatose,") when we appear but they wake up long enough to make a tasty quattro formaggio pizza. It looks like they have live music there in the evenings; maybe the staff pulled a late shift last night. We rouse them again so we can pay our bill and resume our exploration.

We emerge eventually next to a row of incense shops that stand across the road from the Lama Temple complex, which contains over a dozen temples and an impressive 26m tall statue of the Buddha carved from a single sandalwood tree. The faithful are there in numbers and the incense shops must have been doing good business because the aroma fills the air even when you are still some distance from the complex. Despite the crowds, the atmosphere inside is calm and, after admiring the architecture and the huge Buddha, who seems pretty cramped inside his private temple, we sit and people-watch for a while, summoning up energy for the second part of our hutong marathon.

This is to take us across the city to the north of the Forbidden City and then south via connected parkland and lakes. We love strolling through the lanes. Fascinating vignettes of Beijing life are to be found around every corner. A family at dinner outside in an alleyway smile delightfully when they see us watching them. We smile back, embarrassed at having been caught staring. Old women gather together, reviewing recent events at maximum volume, while old men play Chinese chess nearby. Every move is followed by great debate: it always sounds like a fight is about to beak out, but eventually we realise it is just normal conversation. Oblivious to the hubbub, workers sleeping on their break curl up in impossible positions on wooden benches, their shoes ranged neatly beneath them. Others, escaping the heat, squat in the shade of a tree or sip a cold drink outside a food store and gaze at us impassively as we pass.

At the corner of Bancheng Hutong and Nanluogu Xiong, we find a delightful area of cafes and restaurants. Each one has its own style, designed with care, wit, creativity and imagination. One might imagine that they are aiming at a western clientele but far from it. On this warm evening, every establishment is jam-packed exclusively with local customers and we hear, although understand very little of, the distinctive buzz of Mandarin.

We wander around the square between the Drum Tower and Bell Tower, which is a fixture on the package tour circuit, judging by the vast number of bicycle rickshaws lining the streets. We stop for a drink in the Drum and Bell, a backpacker bar/hostel, and then cross into the huge area of parkland that extends all the way down to Tiananmen Square five kilometres away. There are paddle boats on Qianhai Lake and a row of cafes and bars along the west bank on a street called Lotus Lane beckons the hungry and thirsty.

Lotus Lane reminds us of Boat Quay in Singapore and the various eateries there do seem to be set up for tourists. There are plenty of Westerners around and, if we are careless and venture too close to the staff lined up in front of each restaurant, menus are waved at us and we are propositioned in perfect English. We learn to keep our distance and avoid eye contact. At the southern end of the row is a tea shop and we sit outside with tall iced teas watching the boating action on the lake.

The highlight of our walk around Qianhai Lake is a very cool, elderly Chinese man dressed all in white, wearing a large hat, who has parked his bicycle in the shade of a tree. Three small birds are attached by the leg to the handlebars of his bicycle and a fourth bird is hopping around on the ground at his feet. He has set out three money boxes a couple of metres in front of him and a small crowd has assembled to watch.

When someone in the crowd crouches down and proffers a coin, the bird hops over, takes the coin from the person's fingers with its beak, hops off to one of the money boxes and drops the coin in. It then turns to the man in white, who bends and offers it a piece of grain or a seed. The smart little bird is a big hit with the crowd, made up mainly of local couples and groups of girls, and he draws frequent applause and the occasional shrill squeal of excitement. We sit by the water and watch for a while. The little bird's energy never flags. Every time anyone starts to bend a knee, he hops over expectantly, seizes the coin and deposits it expertly, never missing. The man in white doesn't utter a word. A girl crouched next to us explains that this is more than just a game. There is an element of fortune telling going on. Each donor has a question that they want an answer to and the boxes represent three possible answers: yes, no and don't know.

From the eastern edge of the park we venture back into the hutongs and make our way through the area where a sign tells us the stone was cut to build the walls of the Forbidden City, then down to the vast moat that surrounds those walls. There we find people walking their dogs in the cool of late evening and one guy who is fishing in the Forbidden City moat. The scale of the palace that was the home of Ming and Qing emperors for 500 years is enormous and the stroll around the ten-metre-tall walls makes a great precursor to our tour of the interior tomorrow.

From the Forbidden City it is just a short walk back to the hostel but we pause at a small restaurant en route for a quick snack of maopo daofu (spicy bean curd) and gaai laan (Chinese broccoli) and discuss the day. Beijing has captivated us. There are so many aspects of the city that we did not expect. Exploring it involves walking huge distances and staying away from the major traffic arteries is a key strategy. It was wonderful to wind our way through the hutongs, past ancient doorways, gates and courtyards. Despite the fact that many have been modernised with 21st century features such as satellite dishes and solar panels, this takes nothing away from their charm. It was apparent that the hutongs have retained their relevance for both the old people of Beijing who follow the traditional ways and for the new generation of urban Chinese who have transformed some of the lanes to suit their lifestyle.

Beijing: Forbidden City

Where we go inside the huge walls of the city within a city

The next day, we arrive at the Forbidden City at 10am. We should have arrived earlier as the seven hours we then spend exploring its palaces, galleries, alleyways, treasure houses and gardens is not enough to get a true understanding of this incredible place. Later, when we climb to the hill-top temple in nearby Jingshan Park and look down on the roofs of the Forbidden City below, we see huge sections that we have not even touched on, albeit much of the site is closed to outsiders.

It is hard to take in on one visit the sheer scope, variety and rarity of the items on show. There are porcelain, bronzes, jewellery, ornaments, clothing, clocks and mirrors from 3,000 years of Chinese history and the displays represent only a tiny fraction of the collection of artefacts owned by the Palace Museums in the Forbidden City. Some have been passed down from emperor to emperor and dynasty to dynasty, some have been acquired by the State as tribute or by invasion, others have been unearthed by researchers and archaeologists and many have been "donated" by private individuals.

Some of these individuals were key figures in the Communist Party who rescued and protected artefacts of China's cultural heritage from the predations of Mao's Red Guards during the Cultural Revolution. In fact, given the attempt at systematic destruction of the relics of China's imperial past, it is simultaneously heartening to see how much survived and disheartening to imagine the glory of what was destroyed.

To call this palace a city is appropriate. It is enormous and its squares, roads and alleyways easily swallow up the thousands of camera-toting tourists that visit each day. It is very impressive, but we are not thrilled with the automated audio-guide system. The guide recounts some entertaining stories which enhance the tour considerably but, irritatingly, it activates itself from time to time in the wrong places and, in some parts of the palace, decides not to function at all. We conclude that we might have been better off purchasing a good guide book at the same price. There were English-speaking guides touting their services at the entrance but we wanted to be free to choose our own route and schedule.

Spending a whole day there means you either need to bring a picnic or patronise the food and drink outlets inside. These are varied and reasonably priced, apart from the expensive Chinese-branded coffee shop that has replaced the famous Forbidden City Starbucks. There are crowds of visitors around the main buildings on the central strip, which seems to be the route the flag-following groups take, but once you move away from the beaten track to explore the western and eastern buildings and alleys, there are far fewer people around and once or twice we find ourselves completely alone, surrounded by history.

The most-visited buildings have been well-maintained and the fresh lacquer gleams and glows in the midday sun, but, for us, it is equally rewarding to see the more dilapidated areas of the Forbidden City, which must have changed very little since the last emperor moved out and abandoned his home to the curators. In places, the undergrowth is threatening to take over and in one courtyard an unfinished project for a Crystal Palace lays mouldering and rusting away.

While watching the families touring the Forbidden City independently or in groups we notice how a large number of these consist of several adults and one male child who is the primary focus of all the adults' attention and is behaving accordingly. These, of course, are the little princes of the one-child policy and the families are known by the code 4-2-1. That is, four grandparents, two parents, one child. We also remark on a certain haughtiness and disdain on the part of cynical, worldly wise Beijingers towards their starry-eyed rural compatriots.

It is Children's Day in China today, which might explain why there are so many around, and the television is showing news of Premier Wen Jiabo inviting a selected group of ethnic minority children into Zhongnanhai for the day. NBA star Yao Ming is also making celebrity appearances at various events. Many of the children pictured are wearing little red knotted bandannas around their necks to mark the day. It's all very Baden Powell but there is not a woggle in sight.

In the early evening we walk north through Jingshan Park then back through the hutongs to Nanluogu Xiong, the lane of restaurants, cafes and bars that appealed to us so much yesterday. We are once again charmed by the variety and individuality of the establishments and end up going for dinner at a Sichuan place. We eat on the upper terrace while the sun sets over the red and grey tiled roofs of the old city. The restaurant is full of twenty and thirty-somethings meeting up after a day at work and when the bill arrives we find out why. Three good-sized dishes plus drinks come to just 61 Yuan. And the million dollar view comes free of charge.

When we get back to the hotel we collapse, exhausted from our exertions. It is mid-May and hot. Today was the first day that we felt the effects of Beijing's pollution. There was haze in the air all day and the atmosphere was stifling at times.

Beijing: Maosoleum

Where we visit the departed, then depart.

On our last morning in Beijing we decide to visit the Great Helmsman in his "Maosoleum" in the centre of Tiananmen Square. We go unencumbered by bags or cameras to avoid the inconvenience of queuing before and after at the property office. Mao accepts visitors between 8am and midday every day except Monday and, although the queue is long, it moves quickly through ID check (passport required for foreigners), metal detector and water bottle depository, then past the flower and brochure sellers.

We then pass into a reception hall where a white marble statue of Mao gazes over the sea of flowers he has been brought so far today. An old man from the countryside in front of us pauses and starts to bow reverentially to the statue, possibly thinking this is the mummy itself, but a companion grabs his arm and steers him through into the viewing room where Mao himself lies, looking a bit heavy-jowled and glowing bright yellow. He has a red hammer and sickle flag on his chest. In Lenin's tomb we got to walk around three sides of the glass case but here we just pass along the ex-Chairman's left side. The queue moves at quite a pace so we only get about ten seconds of face time with the mummy and quickly find ourselves out and into the souvenir shop.

The old man in front of us is wide-eyed and breathless as he recounts the experience to his companions with a beatific look on his face as if he has just seen a vision of Christ. The encounter has not been quite as impressive for us but we have now seen the two mummies at either end of the Trans-Siberian, so mission accomplished.

We leave the Square and walk east into a very European-looking quarter that is home to a few embassies and the Headquarters of the Tiananmen guard. Columns of officers, both in and out of uniform, are marching in and out of the gates. Every member of one plain clothes squad is wearing an identical outfit of striped collared shirt and beige slacks which makes them instantly recognisable as police officers and seems to defeat the purpose of them being in plain clothes.

We are looking for dim-sum again but even the Cantonese restaurant we find does not serve it, so we head back to the Oriental Plaza again. It is lunch-time when we arrive, the office workers are out and about, the noise in the mall is deafening and there are queues outside every food outlet. So far, we have been fortunate to have only rarely been exposed to the full effect of the mass of the Beijing population in all its glory. When you do find yourself in the presence of such a large volume of people in a confined space, the noise and the crush of humanity can feel oppressive. We will experience a similar feeling later today when we get to Beijing West train station.

To enjoy China to the full, one thing you need to get used to is the intrusion on your personal space. People in the street, in queues, in shopping centres or in stations are not deliberately being offensive or aggressive when they barge into you, so it is wrong to react angrily. Understand that they are simply intent on their own mission in life and just do not notice you. It is as if you are an invisible ghost returned to earth in a Hollywood movie except that passers-by bounce off you rather than glide through you. A person standing next to you will turn and shout at a friend twenty metres away, even though your ear is just centimetres from their mouth. Maybe it is because China's city dwellers are always surrounded by enormous crowds of people and they have lost any sensitivity for the privacy or personal space of others.

Walking back along Wangfujinglu to our hostel, we find the pedestrianised street a little artificial and forced. It's a bit like Main Street in Disneyland; a pastiche of what the city planners imagine a western-style shopping mecca should be. We jump into a taxi to go to the station and the journey is another reminder of the vast scale of Beijing. What looked like a five minute trip on the map takes forty minutes and it is not because of traffic jams or because the driver has chosen a circuitous route. We sweep along vast boulevards which would not look out of place in Los Angeles, lined with modern bank buildings, company headquarters and plush hotels, and finally arrive at the towering bulk of Beijing West itself. As we approach we see the station is surrounded by the usual human debris that all train stations seem to attract, except, this being China, there is just more, much more. We buy lychees from a stall-holder who tries to short change us, then just laughs when we point this out, as if we have joined in on a little joke she is playing on us.

There are no two-person compartments on Chinese trains and we have booked soft-sleeper bunks in a four person compartment. Having felt a little awkward with lower bunks in Russia, we have chosen the upper bunks this time. When we get to our compartment our travelling companions, a middle-aged couple from a small town south of Pingyao, are already installed on either side of the window table. Their sheets are already laid out on their bunks so instead of having other people sit on our beds, as was the case when we last travelled in a four-berth compartment, this time we are in the equally awkward position of sitting on other people's beds. It is only 5pm so still too early to retire to our upper bunks for the night. Anyway there is a speaker in the ceiling blasting out music and the occasional garbled train announcement, so sleep would be impossible. Perhaps we are being too self-conscious, as the Chinese couple do not seem put out at all by our presence and chat easily to us, until our shaky Mandarin-cum-Cantonese runs out and we resort to communicating by occasional smiles.

On reflection, the solution to travelling as a couple in these compartments is to book one upper bunk and one lower bunk on the same side. This means you have control of one side of the table and will not be inconveniencing whatever sleeping plans your companions may have. Neither will they be inconveniencing you. We will make sure we do this in future.

As we come out of the city, we find ourselves rattling along between rolling green hills and, within an hour, we are into the mountains and passing through a succession of tunnels between sheer rock faces occupied only by the occasional goat. I glance at the map and see that this route is not too far away from the railway line we entered Beijing on a few days before. Although we were coming from the North, the line made a long loop before approaching the city from the south-west and we are heading south-west now.

This train differs from the Russian trains we have travelled on in that there is a washroom at one end of each soft-sleeper compartment with three basins in a row and a long mirror. Concerns of privacy take second place to practicality. As in Russia, none of the sinks are fitted with plugs, but here plastic bowls are provided which fit neatly inside the sinks. The toilets themselves are hole-in-the-floor squatters and there is no paper, although there is a water-tap fitted low down on the wall and a small plastic bowl next to it to help you clean up paper-free.

In stark contrast to the assortment of cookies, chocolate, crisps and curled cotton-wool-bread sandwiches served on British trains, here in China the trolley wheeled down the aisle is piled high with fruit : cherries, lychees, apricots, bananas and pineapples, all freshly sealed on white foam trays. This emphasis on healthy eating makes us think of the exercise equipment installed in parks and on street corners all over Beijing, for adults to use to keep fit. It is not uncommon to see people using the equipment at all hours of the day. The older folk we have encountered so far in China all seem to be in great shape. We spent a few minutes the other evening watching a couple who must have been in their late sixties/early seventies playing keep-it-up with a cork and feather shuttlecock. They were extremely skilled and very limber.

We climb up to our bunks at 7pm, not feeling very limber at all. Our legs are sore after all the walking we have done in the past few days. Our roommates take our move as the signal to stretch out and within minutes both are fast asleep with the door wide open and the lights on. We close the door gently, switch off every illumination we can and we are soon out like a light too, lulled to slumber by the rhythm of the train. The beds are wider than on Russian trains and we have real duvets to shield us from the air-conditioning, rather than just blankets in a duvet cover.

Pingyao

Where we experience a living museum and encounter the "Lonely Planet effect".

We are woken by the sun and the wagon attendant comes in five minutes later to return our tickets and tell us we are twenty minutes away from Pingyao. Our travelling companions are still sleeping, so we move out into the corridor as quietly as we can and look out on to a world of small mud-walled villages surrounded by orchards and tidy fields of crops. People are already bent over working in the fields even at this early hour. The train pulls in slowly and only one couple disembarks with us.

It is a quick stop. By the time we reach the platform exit, the train has already pulled out with a loud blast on the horn. We walk over a piece of waste-ground in front of the station, wake up a guy sleeping on a motorised tricycle and are quickly on our way through empty streets heading east towards the ancient walled town that lies at the heart of this city of half a million people.

By a series of fortuitous circumstances, Pingyao has managed to survive the ravages of China's 20th century political upheavals as an almost perfectly preserved Qing Dynasty town. It is a living, breathing, working museum and a UNESCO World Heritage site. The coach parks and lines of souvenir shops outside the walls are evidence of its status as a major attraction for Chinese tourists.

At 5.45 in the morning, before any of the shops have opened and before any other visitors have arrived, the only people up and about, apart from us, are the old ladies sweeping the streets with their reed whisks and wicker baskets. We roll in on our tricycle through the west gate into Pingyao, feeling like we have time-travelled back into ancient feudal China.

Our hostel is a Qing Dynasty wooden courtyard house, quaint and picturesque, with an eaved bell-tower astride the lane beside it. Our room key is on the counter waiting for us when we arrive but there is no-one awake to check us in so we go to our room and get a couple of hours more sleep. The courtyards we cross to get to our room are full of painted screens, red lanterns, sculptures and water fountains.

Later we go out to explore the town. Pingyao's fame initially derived from the fact that it was the headquarters of China's first ever bank. It was a very wealthy town and had a thriving business community in 19th century Qing times. Then the world changed and it became a sleepy rural backwater. Now, with the architecture restored to its former glory, tourism provides a livelihood for many of the townspeople and the wonderful wooden buildings that used to be home to government officials, financiers and merchants are now hostels, restaurants and shops.

Many have been opened up as exhibits to show how people lived and worked in a small affluent Chinese town 150 years ago. It works like a museum with many rooms, each housing a different exhibit, except that here the "rooms" are individual buildings. You can explore the famous bank, opulent residences owned by prominent families of the era and buildings housing other related enterprises that grew up around the bank, such as security companies, accountancy firms and pawn shops. All the exhibits are fitted out with original furniture and make you feel as if it was only yesterday that people were using these rooms and courtyards as homes and offices. There are also a dozen temples, including two dedicated to Guan Di and one huge temple complex dedicated to Confucius, which contains an examination school.

The visitor handling process in Pingyao is curious. Our hostel is inside the old town but we have to go to the ticket office outside the walls in order to buy an entry pass for all the historical buildings, including the hostel we have just left. This is fair enough. After all, we imagine most visitors will come to Pingyao on day trips or stay in the modern city outside the walls. However, when we try to get back into the old town, we find we are not allowed to re-enter via the gate we have just emerged from. A morose young man explains that, now we have tickets, we have to enter via the official visitors' entrance, a damp urine-perfumed tunnel underneath the North Gate. He shrugs apologetically, as if to say that he knows how daft this is, but it is his job to enforce the rules.

Now back inside the old town, we climb the stairs at the North Gate and walk around the top of the walls to the South Gate, a distance of about four kilometres. The walls are ten metres high and five metres wide at the top. They are made of packed earth covered with bricks, which in many places bear a Ming Dynasty stamp, showing that they have been there since long before the town found its moment of fame.

As we stroll, we look down through the battlements onto the dry moat outside the walls and watch the day-to day activities going on around the single storey houses inside. Only a small part of the old town is wooden buildings and tourist strip. Most of it is just ordinary homes and businesses which, although far less romantically picturesque, are still fascinating and evocative of old China. We pass a group of toddlers at play and are amused to see that they are all wearing trousers deliberately slit down the middle at the back to facilitate number twos. Very practical, we think, but also very funny to see them running around with their bottoms hanging out of their pants.

No-one else is around on the top of the walls except one caretaker-cum-souvenir seller dozing next to his wares at each of the towers we pass. They wake briefly when they hear us approach but we are obviously not the target market. They just give us a quick glance, then tug their cloth cap a little lower over their eyes and resume their slumber.

We inspire similar reactions elsewhere. One guy who rents bicycles near our hostel, spends his day lying comatose beneath an awning. We walk past him several times and, on each occasion, he raises his head slightly to call out a strained "hello" and waves his arm in the vague direction of his bikes. This seems to be some kind of automatic reflex rather than a half-hearted display of entrepreneurial zeal. We sense that if we showed any interest we would be causing him immense inconvenience, so we shake our heads each time and he collapses back into his coma with what sounds like a sigh of relief.

We visit one of the temples in town and a monk stops me, grabs my right hand and uses a red felt pen to put three dots at the end of my life lines. He then measures the distance with a small brass plate, marks the plate and tells me I will have a long life. He says if I want to keep the plate, I should give him thirty Yuan but I decline with a smile. He is gracious, takes the plate back and wipes it clean ready to be deployed again.

Having not seen more than a couple of foreign visitors in town all day, we return to our hostel to find the place is full of them, playing pool and ping-pong, watching a movie, playing on computers or having a beer in the bar. We speculate that this may be a manifestation of a phenomenon that we call "the Lonely Planet effect." We have chosen this hostel because it is written up favourably in the Lonely Planet Guide to China. Perhaps others have done the same. To test our theory we go out into town for dinner and deliberately pick the only restaurant mentioned in the Guide. Sure enough, all the other diners are foreigners. We must have passed twenty hostels in the Pingyao old town and at least three times that number of restaurants, all of which are yawning empty. Foreign visitors are gathered in those few places that Lonely Planet recommends.

This may seem blindingly obvious. The influence of Lonely Planet is evidently very strong. However, it seems to us that this has both pros and cons. The main advantage is that people are drawn to places where they will find like-minded fellow travellers and where the staff is used to dealing with "Lonely Planet types", which should ensure a comfortable experience for all concerned. The main drawback is that, given that Guide space and the author's time are both limited, there may well be other establishments that are equally good or better than those featured, but the author did not have time to visit them or space to include them.

If they are not in the Guide, they become virtually invisible and will not even appear on a traveller's radar screen. The businesses therefore suffer accordingly and independent travellers find themselves herded together and not as independent as they may like to think they are. There is also the issue of objectivity. The huge boost to business that a mention in the Lonely Planet Guide confers must give rise to at least the offer of inducements and side-benefits to authors, which in turns calls into question the authenticity of their recommendations. Having said all this, Lonely Planet hasn't steered us wrong yet.

Day two in Pingyao dawns hot and sunny. We buy two tickets for a bus to Xian tomorrow, book accommodation online and then resume our tour of the old town, starting in the old local Government headquarters next door to our hostel. Like most of the places we have seen here, the buildings and gardens have been magnificently restored and maintained, but the museum exhibits within are haphazardly laid out and poorly cared for. However, it is the architecture and landscaping that fascinate us most and these are glorious.

Later we visit a Taoist temple and are surprised to find a bizarre scenario taking place. Five teenage girls in a disco dance group are practising their moves. The courtyard they are bouncing around in is redolent of incense and must normally be an oasis of peace. Not today: massive speakers in one of the temple buildings are blasting out dance music and the atmosphere could not be more out of tune with the normal function of the place. The girls are having a great time though and nobody seems to mind.

We also look around the large former residence of a senior bank official, which features what they call cave-style rooms, built following a traditional northern Chinese design. The rooms stay cool in summer but retain heat in winter, enabling people to survive in spite of extreme seasonal temperatures.

In another of the sites, the courtyard which housed China's first bank, we see photographs dating from the early 1990s that show the massive amount of restoration that was needed then to bring all these buildings back to something like their former glory after more than a century of decay. They must have worked quickly. By 1997 Pingyao was sufficiently restored to earn recognition as a World Heritage site.

When we return to the hostel, staff and guests are crowded around a TV in the lobby. Today is June 4th, 2009, the 20th anniversary of the bloody denouement to the 1989 student protests in Tiananmen Square. The BBC World News channel is showing footage from that night as part of its coverage of the anniversary. It is surprising that the BBC news feed has not been blacked out throughout China on this day of all days. No overseas news channels were available on the TV in our room in Beijing earlier this week and the fact that the BBC journalist is covering the anniversary from the privacy of his hotel room, rather than venturing out into the streets, is a good sign that the authorities still impose reporting restrictions. So how is it that footage relating to the most politically charged event in recent Chinese history is being broadcast here uncensored? Perhaps it is because we are in rural China and it is impossible for the authorities to block every satellite feed. Or maybe the technology is inefficient and some signals escape the jammers.

In the evening we treat ourselves to a local specialty of simmering beef and potato with stir-fried broccoli at the quaintly named Pingyao International Financiers Club, which is neither a club nor a financiers' hangout, although I guess our presence this evening does make it international. Then we walk back to our hostel under a full moon through colourful streets illuminated by red lanterns and yellow neon.

The Road to Xian

Where we catch a bus in a very unusual way and experience an unforgettable bathroom break.

Today is a travel day for us as we move from Pingyao to Xian. However, the day turns out to be far from routine. Instead of taking a train we have been persuaded by a sign in the hostel lobby to take a bus, as the trip is shorter and cheaper.

We are up and ready to go by 9am. One of the hostel staff beckons us out and leads us down the street to a guy on a motorised tricycle, who will take us to the bus. We climb aboard, zip out through a gate in the walls and find ourselves in the middle of Pingyao rush hour traffic. In the narrow streets of the old town the tricycle feels like the perfect mode of transport, small, manoeuvrable and nippy. On the wide highways that criss-cross modern Pingyao, with full-size cars and big trucks flying by on all sides, it feels tiny, tinny and painfully under-powered, especially going up hills.

We cross numerous intersections, ignoring whatever the traffic lights are indicating, feeling extremely exposed and vulnerable. Time passes and we seem to be making slow progress and at 9.30, supposedly the time the bus is leaving, we are still on the tricycle. Moreover, instead of heading into the city towards a bus station, we are going in the opposite direction, leaving the city behind and, according to the signs, heading for the motorway. Quizzing the driver, we discover that the bus to Xian doesn't actually go through Pingyao. It is a direct inter-city service from Taiyuan that just passes by on the motorway. The plan, apparently, is to get to the nearest toll booth, lie in wait for the bus there, flag it down as it slows and jump aboard.

This sounds fine until we actually arrive at the toll booth and take up our position, ready to ambush the bus. There is a police roadblock across the road and, no sooner have we arrived than an officer strolls over, tells our driver that he can't wait there and moves us on. So off we go, back down the highway, back the way we have come, with the driver throwing worried glances over his shoulder at the toll booth plaza which is receding into the distance behind us.

Once we are out of sight of the police, he crosses back over the central divider, stops on the side of the road and, with a quick unconvincing nod of reassurance to us, jumps off the tricycle and runs up the bank, so he can see the toll plaza. We look at each other and shrug our shoulders. Should plan A fail, as it seems it will, as long as we are on the tricycle we always have a ride back into town, where we can come up with a Plan B. There is no traffic on the slip road we are on and without the noise of the tricycle engine in our ears, there is almost complete silence. The only sign of life is an old lady, sitting in the middle of the highway, on the kerb of the lane divider, drinking tea. Anywhere else in the world, she would look out of place; here her presence seems completely normal.

A shout alerts us to the sight of our driver pounding down the bank towards us. We guess correctly that he has seen the bus. He leaps aboard, fires up the engine and we charge back up the road towards the motorway with the driver leaning on his horn and us waving frantically out of both sides of the tricycle to try to attract the attention of the bus, which is already on the approach to the toll booth. We fly past the police roadblock without stopping but think we have missed our chance when suddenly the bus turns, makes a full 360 degree loop around the toll plaza and comes to a stop. The door opens and the bus-driver descends to open the baggage compartment as we pull up next to him. He waves aside our proffered tickets, we fling our bags into the bus and bundle up the stairs with a quick wave of gratitude to our relieved tricycle driver.

We sink into our seats on the almost empty bus, the adrenalin slowly seeps away and we take in the view. Our first impressions of the countryside are factory chimneys jutting skywards from a haze of heat and pollution and broken villages surrounded by immaculately tended fields. Something that strikes us quickly is that not a single scrap of land that could be cultivated has been left untouched. Hillsides have been cut for terraces and orchards of fruit trees occupy dry river beds and highway intersections. Fields of crops stretch to a range of mountains on the horizon to the east and, to the west, sandy scrub-covered ravines gradually flatten out into a cultivated plain.

Two hours into the journey, the bus makes a bathroom stop at what looks at first sight like a western-style motorway service station. The resemblance ends, however, when I enter the men's toilet and find that, although there is plumbing for urinals attached to the wall, the urinals themselves are absent. In their place are a row of six large wooden buckets, all nearly full to the brim. Each bucket has a long queue in front of it and every person takes their turn to try to get as much into the bucket as possible. Of course, they fail and succeed only in splashing it all out onto the floor and onto their shoes. Sofie has a similarly discomfiting experience in the ladies. Some of the cubicles have no doors and there are no locks on those cubicles that have doors, so she finds herself on several occasions face to face with women going about their business. They don't seem to mind but Sofie emerges fearing that she will be traumatised by the experience forever.

Half an hour later, back on the bus, one of our fellow passengers leans over and confides that we are just about to cross the Yellow River and we look out of the window on to a massive, muddy, flood plain looming ahead of us. The far bank of the river is invisible from the near side but, as we cross the bridge, we find that this is not only because the river is so wide but because huge industrial plants on the south bank are throwing up great quantities of smoke into the air, obliterating the horizon. Reading in advance about the environmental catastrophe that has been created as a by-product of China's economic development does not prepare you for the appalling reality. At least the wide torrent of the Yellow River is in motion. We have crossed a number of smaller waterways on our journey today that have not resembled rivers at all, just black sludge lying stagnant and motionless between barren, garbage-strewn banks.

When the view gets too ugly we turn our attention to the old Schwarzenegger movie that is running on the bus video or close our eyes and think ahead to Xian.

Xian

Where we are tested by the challenges posed by a modern Chinese city and survive.

Our inter-city coach arrives in the outskirts of Xian ahead of schedule and, with the invaluable help of a fellow traveller, who is returning home after a business trip, we manage to get on the right bus into the city centre and it drops us at the main railway station close to the old city walls. Our hostel is not far away but in the cloying humidity and unforgiving heat of the afternoon, and with the throng of people on the streets, the walk seems to take hours. We arrive dusty, sweaty and tetchy and are delighted to find that the hostel is something of an oasis. It is in a compound that was previously the Headquarters of the Chinese Communist Party's Eighth Route Army, during the period when the Communists and the Republicans postponed their civil war to fight together in the second Sino-Japanese War from 1937 to 1945.

Later, we go out to explore the city. It is a Friday evening and, as soon as we poke our heads out of the hostel, all our senses are assaulted by the intense noise and ceaseless bustle of this insanely crowded city. Xian has a population of 4 million and it feels like they have all decided to go out on the town tonight. Buses are lined up nose to tail along the main avenues. Cars are trying to make progress past them by mounting the pavements but they are thwarted and brought to a standstill by the huge volume of pedestrians.

Music blares into the streets from every shop and we duck into a restaurant to try to gain some respite from the chaos but have difficulty hearing each other across the table, such is the noise level in the place, which is jammed with diners.

Xian and its people may be loud and busy but we actually feel quite at home here. From the moment we boarded the bus into town, when one man made sure we were heading in the right direction and unnecessarily paid for our tickets, and another gave up his seat so that Sofie could sit down, we have felt welcome. Sofie is particularly happy because she has succeeded in having a chat on the bus in Mandarin with a visitor from Inner Mongolia, which mimicked almost completely a conversation from the book she is studying.

Although nobody outside our hostel seems to speak any functional English at all, everybody has a ready smile. We draw stares as we walk through the streets and we get the impression that the people of Xian are not used to seeing foreigners, but we are left alone completely. Nobody harasses us or tries to sell us anything. The city of Xian itself is not a major tourist destination. The big draw here is the Terracotta Army but the site is a long way out of town. Most visitors probably just pass through behind the darkened glass of tour buses.

As we have remarked frequently on this trip along paths untraveled, it is nice to be in places where foreigners are not automatically seen as tourists and therefore targets. It is a sad fact that, in areas that are used to tourists, not only in China but all over the world, many of the people you meet are only friendly because it is their job and because they want to sell you something. The person you fall into a chance conversation with may take a while to get round to it but eventually the sales pitch will come.

Experience as a traveller teaches you to deal with this phenomenon in one of two ways. You either reject every approach by avoiding eye contact and raising a hand in outright rejection or you smile and chat casually through the preamble ready to say "no", often repeatedly, when the pitch finally arrives. We deploy both tactics depending on our mood or the level of harassment we have been exposed to during the day. The first option, outright rejection, is not as rude as it may first appear. After all, the people approaching you are working and, if you are not going to buy what they are selling, at least you are not wasting their time and they can move quickly on to another target. The alternative option is less offensive but it does tend to give sellers the false expectation that you might be a customer, which is why it is often difficult to get them to accept "no" as an answer once they have spent valuable time trying to make the sale. Adopting the second approach, however, does enable you to experience delightful encounters such as those we had on the bus earlier today with people whose only agenda was to do something for a stranger in need, unsolicited and without any thought of reward. We are very happy that we did not just brush them off when they approached us.

We take it easy on our first full day here, resisting the urge to rush out and see the tombs. Yes, tombs in the plural: there is more than one world-class ancient burial site near Xian. We have been impressed by this city and want to get to know it a little better. We replenish our food stocks in an enormous, eye-popping, three-storey supermarket, buying everything we need for breakfast and picnic lunches over the next three days as well as some supplies for our next overnight train journey down to Guilin.

The streets of Xian are not much less chaotic in the middle of the day than they are in the evening. Every intersection is manned by two sets of policemen, one set in blue, the other in green. The cops in green seem to have a specific traffic control function and they communicate with the world by screeching blasts on a whistle clenched permanently between their lips and hysterical, manic flag-waving. You would think that the combination of such a large police presence, plus traffic lights and walk/don't walk signs, would produce some sort of order but, amusingly for the casual observer, this is not the case. Apparently, a red traffic light can be ignored by the following categories of road-user: rickshaw drivers, cyclists, scooter riders, motorcyclists, tricycle jockeys, important people in big black cars, people in smaller cars of any colour who think they are important, taxi drivers and bus drivers.

This means that even when the green "Walk" light is showing, pedestrians need to inch across the road carefully and with senses set to maximum alert. Even if the larger vehicles are stationary, they may just be a screen concealing a flying scooter or speeding rickshaw. Everyone ignores the cops in green with the whistles and the cops in blue just stare at the chaos impassively, presumably waiting for the inevitable accident to take place and give them something to do.

We go to buy our train tickets for Guilin and are once again amazed by the vast mass of humanity that Chinese railway stations attract. In Xian, the station lies just beyond the old north wall of the city at a point where the wall has been breached by two extended arches running the entire 200-metre length of the vast concourse. Hundreds of people are massed under the arches and every scrap of shade is occupied. There are hundreds more on the other side of the concourse, lying, squatting or sitting in the shadow cast by the station walls.

Our destination is the sound and fury of the ticketing hall, where we do pretty well and find the right queue at our second attempt. We wait patiently, rehearsing what we are going to ask for and trying to anticipate what the clerk will say in reply. Our turn comes and we move forward confidently, smiles at the ready. The clerk looks up, sees us, shrieks, gets to her feet and runs away. Our smiles disappear. There is a slight delay and a new clerk appears, takes her seat and bends towards her microphone. "Good afternoon, how may I help you?" she says in perfect English. We persist in trying to use the phrases we have learned but the clerk's English is a very welcome safety net. Ten minutes later we emerge, tickets in hand. Hostels and hotels will buy tickets for their guests and this saves you having to go to the station booking office yourself, but they do charge a fee for the service and it does mean you miss out on an opportunity for a little unique interaction.

If you are reading this with a view to following in our footsteps, we would recommend taking the plunge every time. Even if there is no English-speaking clerk on duty, if you have done a little online research on train times, numbers and seat options, have a few words in Mandarin and can summon up a little courage, you will find it is not as hard as you may have thought to book your own tickets. Take your time when you are at the desk and be assured that the clerk is trying just as hard as you are to make sure you get what you want. Don't leave until you have double-checked the tickets thoroughly. Don't worry. If, despite all your precautions, you end up getting on a train going somewhere you didn't know you wanted to go, sitting on a wooden bench among the chickens, just enjoy the ride. That's what travelling is all about.

Xian: Han Yanling

Where we spend a day visiting a magnificent archaeological site in Xian that is not the Terracotta Army.

A Sunday in Xian and we decide to spend the day visiting a place we have read a lot about, the Han Yanling Museum at the site of the tomb of Han Dynasty emperor Jingdi. The site is twenty kilometres out of town just off the road to the airport. It turns out to be an absolutely world class museum and one of the major highlights of our whole trip but for some reason it is hard to get to and is not included in any of the popular tourist itineraries.

The usual advice for those wanting to visit Han Yanling is to hire a taxi driver, but we don't fancy paying a taxi driver to sit around for a few hours while we go exploring, so we ask around and find out that the number 4 bus goes there. So all we have to do is find a bus stop with a no. 4 bus schedule posted and wait there until a no. 4 bus comes along.

If only the Xian bus system were so simple. We end up finding a bus before we find the bus stop and chase him through the slow traffic until he and we get to a stop simultaneously. The bus is empty so we have a chance to speak with the ticket seller at some length as we pay. We tell him where we are going and he tells us we have to take two no. 4 buses to get there, which is a little confusing, but we decide just to go with the flow and see what transpires.

The trip is entertaining. Not only do we have the benefit of a soundtrack of western opera being blasted out on the bus speaker system, a slow-moving bus turns out to be an excellent vantage point from which to watch suburban Xian prepare for the day. First, we see a long line of people waiting in front of a cinema, not unusual in itself, but it is strange to see a movie queue forming at 9 o clock in the morning. Next, we notice a chef on a restaurant forecourt briefing his staff, all lined up at ease in parade formation. This is evidently standard practice as a few minutes later we watch a hotel manager doing the same in the car park with his troops.

It is also on this journey that we finally decode the meaning of the long blasts on the horn that many drivers tend to deploy here. They don't mean "Look out!" or "I'm coming through", as you might guess. Rather they are an expression of annoyance and mean, "You made me brake!" Whenever another road user inconveniences him in any way, our opera-loving bus driver expresses himself by leaning on the horn for a full fifteen seconds.

We pass into the northern suburbs of Xian and arrive in a residential district where there is a lot of building going on. There are huge wall posters carrying enticing advertisements for yet-to-be-constructed housing estates with grand names like Royal Landscape, Park Living and Elegant Sky. The idea is evidently to entice prospective purchasers with the illusion that they will be moving to an exotic, green oasis of calm and peace in the middle of the dusty grey city.

Xian is a city on the move. In the city centre, streets are divided by walls of tin that hide the construction work for a metro system. Pavements are obstructed by scaffolding, construction sites expand into the roads forcing pedestrians into the traffic and lines of cranes punctuate the skyline to the horizon.

Our bus pulls to a halt on the side of the road opposite one of the apartment projects. A couple of other buses are already parked here. A small bus-washing service is evidently in operation here although five of the bus washers are on a break when we arrive. They are squatting on the kerb, mops across their laps, eating rice with a couple of bus drivers, necks craned over their bowls. Our ticket collector motions us to descend and directs us to another no. 4 bus parked a few metres away. It is empty except for a lady with a mop so we follow the local custom and squat on the kerb to wait for something to happen.

We don't have to wait long. After all, this is Xian, home of the most hospitable, friendly people in China. A young man comes over, asks us if we are going to Han Yanling and, between his poor English and our worse Mandarin, we gather that the bus we are sitting next to will be leaving in twenty minutes. He points out that the front panel on this no. 4 bus is painted green while the front panel on the no. 4 bus we arrived on is blue. Green highlighted no. 4 buses travel between this housing estate and the Han Yanling site while blue highlighted no. 4 buses go between here and the city centre. Now we understand.

Our second no. 4 bus of the day whisks us off to Han Yanling and we are there in fifteen minutes. We are impressed by the museum from the moment we swing off the highway onto a smooth, wide drive surrounded on all sides by acres of rose gardens in full bloom. It looks glorious and our hopes for the day, already high, climb still further. They are to be exceeded.

Two main attractions compete for visitors' attention here. There is a museum, which contains artefacts recovered from the ten satellite pits to the north-east of the Emperor's tomb mound that have so far been excavated.

The other attraction is an underground observation centre, about 500 metres away, that has been constructed over and around the pits themselves. This means that you can see some objects presented effectively and intelligently in a spacious, sensitively designed setting, with labels and descriptions in several languages, and other objects left in the pits exactly as they were found. Many are still half-buried in the earth where they were originally placed over two thousand years ago. The pits are three storeys below present ground level and are covered by glass walkways so you can look down and see everything in the minutest detail, despite the low lighting levels required to preserve the artefacts as well as possible.

The ten pits that have been opened have revealed thousands of clay, bronze and iron artefacts, all buried next to the emperor's tomb mound in order to recreate a world after death that would mimic the imperial court in life. In most cases, the artefacts are representations in miniature. There are hundreds of fifty-centimetre tall human clay figures, which were originally clothed in silks and satins, although these have long disintegrated. They are finely modelled, the heads individually moulded with astonishingly realistic features and expressions. Character shines from each chiselled face. In one of the pits, the earth has been cleared down to shoulder level, so all you can see are the heads jutting out; line after line, column after column, arranged in eternal formation waiting forever to be called into service by their long-dead emperor.

Both the museum and the underground facility are of the highest quality. No expense has been spared to ensure that visitors have the closest possible access to a unique historical perspective. The structures have been designed so that their environmental impact is minimal. The building housing the underground pits is invisible until you are right on top of it. As you approach, no part of it disturbs your clear view of the neighbouring tomb mound.

The whole place is a technological marvel and it is evident that it has been created by people who are proud to share this window on a long lost world. It is also clear that this is a project that has much, much more to offer. Scans have revealed that there are a further 71 pits radiating out from the tomb mound, about twenty on each side. Then there is the Emperor's tomb itself, lying somewhere under the mountain of earth that rises from the plain. This is a hill rivalled locally in height only by the tomb mound of his Empress a few hundred metres away. The burial site as a whole covers 67 hectares and it will be generations before all its secrets are revealed. It is tantalising to imagine what wonders will be discovered, especially when you see what amazing things have been found already in the comparatively small area that has been exposed to date.

The sensitivity of the Chinese approach to this project is evident in the intelligence and sophistication of the museums and the fact that visitors are welcomed with open arms but not sought out for commercial gain. They know that they are unlocking a unique historical treasure trove and that future generations will regard this site as one of the wonders of the world. It is a task that even now, after thirty years of research, is just beginning.

The bus journey back is the reverse of the morning trip and we eventually arrive back in Xian just as a thunderstorm is about to hit the city. Xian gets fifty centimetres of rain a year and a good few of these are about to fall, turning the sandy streets, parks and construction sites into mud and making the umbrella sellers, who have suddenly appeared out of nowhere, a little richer.

We take shelter in a small restaurant where once again we manage to eat well and cheaply from a menu on which we understand absolutely nothing. This is one of the most useful skills we have developed on our travels. It involves a lot of smiling and pointing, not to mention a considerable degree of tolerance on the part of the restaurant staff and our fellow diners, whose food we are pointing at.

When the rain eases off we stroll back to the hostel, taking a damp detour through a lovely city park. The pagodas in the gardens have been colonised by amateur singers and musicians and their supporters so, as we wander past rain-misted willows overhanging a small lake, the perfect atmospheric soundtrack accompanies us. As I said before, we like Xian and are very happy that we have added an extra day to our stay here.

Xian: Bingmayong

Where we spend a day visiting a magnificent archaeological site in Xian that is the Terracotta Army.

On our third day in Xian we have a date with Emperor Qin's Terracotta Army, or Bingmayong as it is referred to in China. This time the journey is much more straightforward. We just have to find Workers Vanguard Bus 306 outside the train station ticket hall, pay the fare of 7 Yuan each and we are on our way. The trip takes an hour and if you sit on the right hand side of the bus you get a good view of the Li Shan mountain range as well as Emperor Qin's tomb mound, which is the big hill on its own about a mile before you get to Bingmayong.

There is no missing the stop. An enormous coach park and rank upon rank of souvenir shops await our arrival in what has become one of the top tourist attractions in China. This is already a very different atmosphere from the tranquillity and reverence of the Han Yanling site. There are huge new commercial complexes springing up all around the entrance and exit to capture the attention and credit cards of the millions of visitors that flock here from all over the world. Plenty of people are around today, a sunny Monday in June, but the place is obviously set up to accommodate tens of thousands of tourists a day, entertain them, amaze them, feed them and empty their wallets.

Our first reaction, therefore, is one of disappointment and during our visit we find other aspects of the experience that we think could be improved. However, we do not leave disappointed. The magnificent positive of the main draw at Bingmayong is so huge that it dwarfs any negatives. The soldiers of the Terracotta Army are lined up in the huge pits where they were placed over 2,000 years ago to accompany the Emperor who first unified China into his life after death. Having excavated sections of three pits so far, the archaeologists have left other sections undisturbed, as scans have shown that their contents are the same. That is, fragments of clay warriors and horses shattered by the collapse of the roof timbers which originally provided a ceiling for the pitch-black, paved corridors in which they stood. The lines of warriors have been painstakingly reconstructed from the fragments and this is an incredible achievement.

Before visiting the pits, acting on advice from friends who have been there before us, we head first to the cinema to the left of Pit One and watch the short film that they have running on a continuous loop there. The film does an excellent job of introducing visitors to what they are about to experience and places the Army in its historical context. It depicts the huge scale of the work involved in building the tomb and its satellite pits and describes how, shortly after they were closed, the pits were ransacked by looting rebels looking for weapons. After the movie, we move on to Pit Three, then Pit Two, leaving Pit One, the **pièce de résistance,** for last.

An independent display in a building to the right of the main entrance features half-life-size models of two bronze chariots, each drawn by four bronze horses. These were found in a small pit twenty metres away from the tomb mound. They are beautiful, intricate works of art, created by artists over 2,000 years ago in astonishingly minute detail and they alone would be worth the entrance fee. They are absolutely unique, utterly priceless and truly wonderful to see.

As at Han Yanling, the thought of how much else there is still to uncover here takes the breath away. There are 1.5 kilometres of meadow between the Army pits and the tomb mound. Minor excavations elsewhere in the area have unearthed not only the bronze horse-drawn chariots but other animals and birds cast in bronze. Writing not long after the death of Emperor Qin, historian Sima Qian described the tomb mound as a reconstruction of the living world with rivers and oceans of mercury.

Bingmayong dates from 1979, when the concept of the museum receiving millions of foreign visitors a year would have seemed impossible. China was just emerging from the chaos of the final Mao years and the brief interregnum of the Gang of Four. Deng Xiaoping was in charge but the country had not yet opened up to the outside world.

The site is showing its age. The design is clunky and antiquated and there is little sign that it has been updated over the last thirty years. The Terracotta Army has become something of a theme park attraction, populated by megaphone-wielding tour parties and infested by persistent unofficial souvenir sellers masquerading as visitors, who peddle trashy mementos from plastic carrier bags.

After experiencing the sophistication, sensitivity and intelligence of the Han Yanling facility, the clumsiness and carelessness of Bingmayong leaves us a little dismayed. We recognize that the gulf in class between the two museums is probably just a reflection of the huge progress China has made in the last quarter of a century. However, we are left with the impression that once World Heritage status was assured and millions of visitors were guaranteed, the creative and talented people moved on (to Han

Yanling?), leaving the site in the hands of those whose primary aim is to derive commercial profit from the facility, rather than improve it technologically, artistically or culturally.

The captions on the exhibits are pointless and merely state the obvious or make a crass political point, such as the claim that chemical analysis of the weapons found in the pits suggests that the Chinese developed chrome plating 2,000 years before the Americans. This leaves visitors reliant on the half-truths, fabrications and clichés peddled by the tour guides.

One of the legends of the Terracotta Army is that two brothers found the first pieces while they were sinking a new well. The location of the well is visible on the edge of Pit One. But as John Man points out in his excellent book on the subject, (a great companion for any visit to Bingmayong), local people always knew that there was something substantial down there. Artefacts had been unearthed in the past to be sold quietly and the brothers and their neighbours must have encountered the impenetrable brick-tiled floor of the pits a number of times in the course of attempting to sink previous wells. This was why they chose to sink this particular well at the point where the obstruction ended and they could get down to the water table.

Fortunately on this occasion they told a local archaeologist of their finds and it was equally fortunate that he decided to report the finds to his superiors, who passed the news all the way up to the new national leadership team in Beijing. They seized on the Terracotta Army as an ideal opportunity to advertise to the world the past glories of a newly open and resurgent China.

One thing is certain; the local farmers no longer have to dig wells for their water. Their village has turned into a small city - a city with one very profitable industry - and it is hard to begrudge them their good fortune. All in all, the Terracotta Army is an incredible thing to witness and none of the commercial trappings of the site can dilute its impact or importance. We have a great time, the sun shines all day and the well-tended gardens around the museum are a lovely place for a picnic.

The local bus drops us back in Xian and we decide to explore a little more of the city. This time we set off towards the south with the aim of working our way down to Dayanta, the Big Goose Pagoda, in time for a musical fountain show which takes place there at 9pm every evening and which sounds like fun. Near the south gate we find a historical quarter running parallel to the wall where there are rows of old buildings housing shops selling jade, calligraphy, brushes, ink and other artists materials. It is a very tranquil part of town and seems to be somewhere you could pleasurably idle away a few hours. However, we have a mission and we are hungry so we move on.

As it turns out we enjoy our dinner so much we come out of the restaurant to find ourselves with insufficient time for the six-kilometre walk to Dayanta. We can't find the correct stop for a bus to take us down there so we decide to take a motorised tricycle, which of course means we need to deploy our negotiation skills. The first driver we approach asks for thirty Yuan. We think this is too much and eventually choose a lady driver who agrees to take us there for fifteen Yuan. We settle back in the tricycle thinking we have done well until, that is, we hear her boasting of her windfall to every other driver she encounters on the way. She proves to be well worth the money, however. We are in the hands of a true Queen of the Road. She accelerates fast and stays at top speed all the way. The only time she touches the brakes is when a truck swings suddenly across our path and, even then, her hesitation is only momentary. She is happy with the deal she has struck and we are too. We arrive at

Dayanta ten minutes before the show. We see at once that we will not be alone.

The huge square is crowded with what must be several thousand city folk out enjoying this warm Spring evening. Some are sitting expectantly around the multiple fountains laid out on terraces below the floodlit pagoda. Others are strolling along tree-lined avenues that flank the square. The atmosphere is festive and we are impressed that a daily event can draw such a throng. Exactly on the stroke of 9 the show begins. It is a riot of music, colour and choreographed water spouts but the best entertainment is provided by local teenagers, who are having the time of their lives daring each other to run through the fountains and getting completely soaked in the process. Some of the inadvertent drenchings are hilarious and everyone has a great time for the twenty minutes that it lasts.

As we leave, we stop at a Baskin and Robbins on the edge of the square to buy a sorbet and while we are in the shop we notice again how much attention we are getting. We have spotted other Europeans in Xian but there are obviously few enough for people to turn and stare or point us out to their friends. It is not unpleasant but it does suggest that, off the track beaten by organised tour groups, Westerners are still an unusual sight in China.

We make another tricycle driver's day by offering her 15 Yuan to take us back into the city centre and we ask her to drop us off at a night market that has taken over a pedestrianised street a couple of blocks south of the Bell Tower. There, we join the crowds of shoppers picking their way between stalls and stepping carefully over the sheets laid on the pavement by ground-level vendors. Clothing and accessories are the main themes and the market is thriving, with plenty of haggling, buying, selling and trying on happening everywhere we look. We have a great time watching all the activity; yet another aspect of this big, friendly, crazy, hyperactive city to enjoy and remember.

On Day 5 in Xian, our last, we finally stumble upon the city's tourist district, an area known as the Muslim quarter, which is the closest thing to an Old Town that remains. Here, for a couple of hundred metres between the Drum Tower and the City Mosque are souvenir sellers noisily hawking the same mass-produced China memorabilia you see everywhere. The restaurants have English menus in the window that feature prices ten times those we have been paying up to now. We pass through quickly, making a mental note not to return that way.

Instead we make for the area by the South Gate that we found yesterday, where the quiet streets provide such a welcome respite from the bustle of the main shopping avenues. We stop briefly for dumplings and noodles and then go back through the centre of the city, looking around some of the department stores and shopping arcades on the way. We find a huge contrast between enormous underground caverns containing hundreds of tiny shops selling everything you can imagine at cheap, cheap prices and multi-storey glass towers filled with expensive, branded, luxury goods, such as Timberland, Converse, North Face and Reebok. As we can see from the price tags, these are the genuine articles, as opposed to the cheap knock-offs we saw on sale last night in the street market only a hundred metres down the road. Nevertheless, there are plenty of people spending money in the expensive outlets, a further sign, as if we needed one, of the new affluence of many of China's urban elite.

Back at the hostel, I sit down at a computer in the bar to write up my daily notes and a large rat runs down the wall and goes behind the desk I am working at. I jump up to see where it has gone, attracting the attention of the barman who comes over to help me. We can't find it but the barman reassures me that I can sit down again without fear of being bitten as the rat must have escaped into the kitchen. Well, that's OK then. We decide to skip breakfast the next morning and eat outside.

The Long Ride to Guilin

Where we have plenty of time to make a close study of travelling by sleeper train in China and come up with some tips and tricks.

Having seen how busy Xian station was when we went there to buy our tickets, we leave early to catch our train. We have carried our camping cooking gas canister on a dozen trains so far on this trip without raising an eyebrow, but we lose it at the Xian station entrance. The cop manning the baggage scanner asks us to remove it, pointing vaguely to a poster on the wall listing prohibited items. We can't see "cooking gas canister" on the list but decide it is futile to argue.

We may be early but so is everyone else. The waiting room looks like an airport lounge when the air-traffic controllers are on strike. It seems that many use a queue-holding strategy, sending a small advance guard to commandeer a section of the seating area and set up camp for the main group who will join them nearer departure time. This means that the folk in this particular waiting room are not all going to be on our train. Some are here for earlier trains, some for trains leaving much later.

We figure out that the way to get a place to sit is to try and spot travellers who are going to take the next train. They will usually be perched on the edge of their seat, eyes fixed on both the station clock and the growing throng forming around the closed departure gate. They are weighing up in their mind at what point they should leave the comfort of their seat and join them. You then hover nearby and try and sidle swiftly into their place when they eventually hop up. You need to be quick, though. A couple of hundred other people in the hall are doing the same thing and your competitors are much more experienced. However, as a foreigner, you do have the advantage of surprise.

We are sitting near the front when the gate opens at 7pm for a 7.22 train and we think we will be among the first to board. We could not be more wrong as everyone speeds past us down the stairs and along the platform and we actually find ourselves among the last to board. Two Chinese ladies are already comfortably ensconced in our compartment when we arrive. We have gone for one upper and one lower bunk on the same side of the compartment this time and early indications are that this will be a less awkward arrangement than two-up or two-down, as it means we have one half of the compartment and they have the other. The ladies are taking this train all the way to Nanning, close to the Vietnamese border. We will disembark before them, in Guilin.

Chinese trains differ from Russian trains in a number of respects. The attendants are less authoritarian, you can switch the lights on and off when you like and the toilets are not locked, so the decision whether to use them when the train is passing through a town or stopped at a station is left to your common sense, good taste and the degree of emergency involved. Having said this, during one stop, at Hengyang, an official in a white coat comes along the platform towards our carriage and this has our attendant scurrying to try and lock the toilet doors. She is too late and some loud shouting ensues. This may suggest that our initial impression was false and that the doors are probably supposed to be locked while the train is in a station.

Soon after you board, the attendant comes in and takes your ticket away in exchange for a small credit card-sized token. When your stop is imminent and she comes in to give you the thirty-minute warning, you return the token and get your ticket back.

We wake at dawn on the train as usual, as the compartment curtains do nothing to keep out the sunlight. Our companions are snoring gently across from us under the standard white duvets they give you in ruanwoche (soft-sleeper) class. Ruanwoche is 4 people to a compartment with a lockable door to the corridor. It costs twice as much as yingwoche (hard-sleeper), which sleeps six to a compartment with no door.

Ruanwoche is the equivalent of first class but it is not first-class by Western or even Russian standards. The attendants may be supposed to lock the toilet doors in the station, as we have learned, but they don't appear to have toilet cleaning on their list of duties, the flushes don't work and no paper is provided. However, the ruanwoche compartments do have a separate washroom with a row of sinks, which means you don't have to clean your teeth in the same room as the toilet. This is a bonus.

In each ruanwoche compartment you are provided with a pair of rubber sandals each, a tablecloth, a metal tea tray, a rubbish bin and a radio. You can adjust the volume of the radio via a black knob under the window but you cannot completely turn it off. There are electrical sockets, but many have burn marks around them. We avoid these, not wanting the train to fry our electronics. There is also a flask of boiling water in the compartment, which you can replenish from the samovar outside the attendant's room.

If you are economising and thinking of travelling yingwoche, bear in mind that the Chinese railways are a mass transit system and therefore you will be accompanied by the masses in transit. There is little or no concept of personal space in yingwoche and your travelling companions will hawk or spit or empty the contents of their nasal passages wherever and whenever the mood takes them. In the morning it is quite a symphony and some guys have developed the skill of noisily regurgitating a lung to a level where it is something of an art form. Be warned.

You do get used to it but, when you first arrive in China, it is easy to be offended when someone hawks close to your ear or spits phlegm past your nose, but it is not meant to offend and no-one will understand if you get upset. While we are on the subject I should add the following to the list of public activities you will need to be prepared to tolerate on trains in China: noisy slurping, studious nose-picking, surgical toe-nail cleaning and people holding conversations at full power with someone twenty metres away at the other end of the crowded carriage. Having said that, the volume will still be the same if they are talking to someone sitting right beside them.

The yingwoche wagons have partitions up to head-height with six places in each of nine partitioned areas. There are no doors and bags are stored on a rack above the corridor. There are folding seats in the corridor under the baggage racks but if you have the bottom bunk, both you and the people on the middle and upper banks will be sitting on it during the day. The corridor lights are left on throughout the night so, without doors or full-length partitions, the sleeping areas are never dark. The only place you can get any privacy is the toilet and there is only one in each hard sleeper wagon, shared by 54 people, so it is constantly in use. However, there does not seem to be any rule saying that you can only use the toilet in your own wagon. Many yingwoche folk use the facilities in the ruanwoche cars.

The restaurant wagon workers regularly come along the corridor pushing trolleys laden with lunchboxes of rice, meat and vegetables so you don't have to pack a picnic for the trip if you don't want to. Other trolleys pass by carrying Chinese magazines, Chinese books and "international" toilet paper.

On the subject of which, here is a guide to using the toilet on Chinese trains. (I include this here because we really wished we had advanced notice of the techniques to deploy, instead of having to resort to trial and many errors.) They are usually hole-in-the-floor-style facilities. First, always wear outdoor shoes, NOT slippers, and definitely avoid going within five metres of the toilet door in bare feet. Next, make sure you don't have anything in the back pockets of your trousers. If something falls out you are unlikely to see it again. Go in and shut the door, locking it if you can. Then, facing the toilet window, (i.e. looking out of the train) place your feet on the two foot-shaped marks in the pan, drop your trousers and pants to just below your knees. Then squat on your haunches, with your butt directly over the hole. Remember to deploy one hand to clutch the crotch of your trousers to stop them coming into contact with the floor of the pan as you squat. A metal bar is bolted into the wall under the window directly in front of you. Hold onto this tightly with your other hand, especially if the ride gets rocky. This is not a place to lose your balance. Toilet paper goes down the hole with everything else. It all ends up on the tracks.

If there is water in the pipes, flush by pushing down on the obvious lever. There is no sneaky, tricky, hard-to-find Russian under-sink-foot-pedal technology here. As I mentioned earlier, the washbasins are in a separate room, usually at the other end of the wagon, and are fitted with normal taps. This means that all surfaces, door handles etc. between the toilet and the washbasin should be treated as if they are toxic. A final note: if you find you have a Western-style toilet option in your compartment, do not rejoice prematurely. Most of your travelling companions will probably squat with their feet on the seat and, in the absence of the metal self-stabilising bar, may not be able to aim very well. Our advice would be to choose the squatter every time.

At mid-morning we cross the Yangtze at Wuhan. This is the last of the great rivers of the world that we will encounter on this trip. Wuhan looks like an interesting, bustling city and we make a mental note to return on a future visit to China. Beyond Wuhan, we enter a different China, a land of bright green fields and bright red earth. Water buffalo drag single ploughs knee-deep through flooded meadows and, for the first time since Warsaw, the countryside we are travelling though is not dry, dusty or sand strewn. We have arrived in Southeast Asia.

Gloriously verdant rice paddies stretch to the horizon and gone are the grey stone huts of the north. The village houses now are two or three storeys, white-plastered or bare redbrick and have red-tiled roofs. Our route will now take us through Hunan Province and on into Guangxi Province. There is water everywhere. The richness of the land takes us by surprise after what we have experienced over the last few weeks.

One of the many joys of train travel is just to gaze from the window of your compartment and observe the vignettes of life taking place beyond the glass. People working in the fields, old men relaxing outside their homes watching the train go by, groups of women chatting by the roadside, children playing: the view is ever-changing. Travelling through cities, the tracks rarely pass through the scenic parts of town but there again, there is value in getting a glimpse of how ordinary folk live in parts of the city that have not been beautified for tourist consumption.

Riding by train, we have been privileged to see much more of the countries we have passed through than if we had connected the dots by plane. Even though we have added 2,000 kilometres to our trip in the Altai and a further 2,000 kilometres in the Gobi, plus side trips to Suzdal and Lake Baikal, and have covered a huge distance in a relatively short time, we have never felt rushed. We have found the experience completely relaxing, especially the 2-person SV compartment on the Baikal, which was as comfortable as a hotel room, albeit a hotel moving at 50 kms/hour.

Guilin

Where we spend a lot of time underground, experience a little singing and dancing, finally reach the end of our journey and start planning the next one.

By mid-afternoon we are well on our way to Guilin, trundling along through the lush valleys of Hunan, under a heavy sky, pregnant with rain, the gloom deepening the emerald green of the landscape. Small, neat villages surrounded by tidy, well-tended fields of corn, cabbages, rice and other crops decorate the plains and hillsides. Every possible square centimetre of land seems to be cultivated.

Coming into Yongzhou, we pass through a range of small hills where large, smooth, white stones litter fields and orchards, lending them a surreal, fairy-tale appearance. It is all very beautiful and our train window offers us the perfect vantage point. Emerging from a gap between the hills, we find ourselves on the bank of a wide river wending its way through overgrown banks and spot a man in a conical hat sitting motionless astride a small jetty. Several sampans are moored there in a timeless image of rural China.

From Yongzhou, the train seems to become more of a local service than an inter-city express and the number of people in the sleeping wagons has thinned out considerably. Some, however, will stay on for a second night, as the train is not scheduled to arrive in Nanning until dawn tomorrow.

We get to Guilin right on time. There is a crowd outside the station but it seems no-one is waiting for us, despite the hostel having insisted they would send someone. Having been warned about aggressive touts and taxi drivers here, we sidle off to one side to call the hostel for directions but, just as we are about to do this, we spot a young couple hanging back from the throng. They turn out to be our meeters and greeters. They attempt to get a taxi for all of us but end up getting into a heated argument with the driver before we set off, (the warnings were spot on), so we take our bags out of the trunk and tell them we are happy to walk to the hostel if it's not too far. They escort us for about a mile up Zhongshan Lu, the main road from the station and find the hostel on the south bank of a wide river.

Guilin is surrounded, percolated and defined by water and we have arrived in the rainy season. The rivers are high, brown and surging and the limestone karst towers and pinnacles that surround and punctuate the city are ghostly in the mist and low cloud. On our first morning in town, we wander along hot, humid streets, cross numerous bridges and finally arrive at our first destination, Seven Stars Park, which is home to seven distinctive limestone peaks and has been a tourist destination for over 1500 years.

We escape from the heat by joining a group of visitors and descending into an enormous cave system that extends for two kilometres beneath the mountains. This is an amazing place with fabulous, beautifully-illuminated ancient limestone formations. We wander away briefly to escape the constant chatter of our guide and enjoy a moment of peaceful contemplation in an enormous domed chamber off the well-trodden route. The moment does not last long before we are discovered and shepherded back to the group. The guide is tirelessly energetic. Most of her excited commentary seems to be focussed on relating the shapes of various stalactite and stalagmite formations to animals or celebrity faces. At one point, she even breaks into song. We can't help but applaud her courage.

A number of professional photographers have set themselves up here and there in the cave to take pictures of people posing in front of particularly photogenic spots. We have seen guys like these in Beijing, Pingyao and Xian and everywhere they seem to be doing good business. You would think, in these digital days of camera phones, it would be difficult to sell holiday snaps but the photographers always seem to have a queue of customers lined up. They dress them up in ancient Chinese costume or pose them reclining in a rickshaw, mounted on a horse or seated on a throne. In just a couple of minutes, a unique, personal souvenir is printed, framed and presented, destined, no doubt, to end up in pride of place in their home, next to the household gods and photos of ancestors.

Leaving the cave, we visit a monster panda that is waiting for us in an enclosure, lying flat on his back with legs apart, his genitals pointing skywards and his focus completely on a bunch of bamboo shoots clutched in his razor sharp claws. He is as far from being the cute, cuddly panda of western myth as you could possibly get. He's a powerful matt black and dirty brown bear with a major screw-you attitude.

We are impressed by a museum in the park featuring a collection of fossils and naturally occurring stones. A lady with excellent English spies us as we enter and takes us under her wing. She shows us black, shiny ink stones from the Yellow River and an amazing collection of Chinese picture jasper or "painting stones" that are patterned with miniature landscapes. But the most impressive exhibits are 250-million-year-old chrysanthemum stones from Hubei, which are formed when pressure embeds mineral crystals in grey limestone. They look as if they have been sculpted by a gifted hand. Also on display is an enormous mammoth tusk and trilobite fossils from 500 million years ago. In the same room are a number of fossilised dinosaur eggs. They are identical to those we saw lying around in the Gobi when we were exploring the cliffs at Bayanzag.

Climbing one of the peaks in the park gives us a view of Guilin's spectacular situation, nestled in the river valley between the encircling green karst mountains. A Buddhist temple at the foot of the peak is a wonderful place to rest after the climb. The smell of incense and the faint pulse of chants and drums emanate from within and are carried on a soft breeze.

As we exit the park, we have to pass a long row of souvenir stalls selling the same collection of colourful crap found everywhere tourists gather in China. We brace ourselves to run the gauntlet but the stallholders are all squatting on the kerb having an afternoon snack so we are spared any harassment. However, once back in town we are not so lucky and it seems that every time we stop or even slow our walking pace a fraction we are approached by someone trying to sell us on a restaurant for dinner or a tour for the next day. It is annoying but we know it's not personal so we do our best to stay patient. Guilin is a popular destination for both foreigners and Chinese. For many local people tourism is their livelihood. The touts are just trying to make a dollar.

Late in the day, as we are crossing the Liberation Bridge over the River Li, we are privileged to witness a couple of "only-in-China" vignettes. First we see a small, wiry man wearing only shorts and flip-flops, who has a massive fridge roped onto the back of his bicycle and is straining, calf muscles popping, to pedal his load up and over the bridge. A colleague at his side on another bicycle is pedalling equally hard, pulling on the fridge-hauler's handlebars in an effort to help him. They look like they are making good progress. A few metres behind them is another cyclist who has an even larger freezer box strapped to the back of his bicycle but, with no-one to help him, he has dismounted and is pushing his load up the incline to the bridge.

Down below, the river is a churning chocolate-coloured torrent with whirlpools around the pillars of the bridge. We gaze casually downstream and spot something splashing in the water a few hundred metres away. As it approaches we see to our astonishment that it is a swimmer, fighting his way upstream. Looking behind him we find a dozen more, doing the same thing and dodging the plastic waste and vegetation carried by the river as it flows past them. Their target is the bridge and as they get closer we can see that these are not young men, but they are incredibly strong swimmers. As each man touches a bridge pillar he stops fighting the river and allows himself to be carried back by the current to a spot on the bank where a group of people are waiting. Not for the first time in China, we are impressed by the physical fitness of the older generation.

At dinner that evening we learn that when a waitress in a Szechuan Restaurant warns you that a dish you have ordered is "hen laat" (very spicy), you should heed the warning and order something else. After dinner, mouth, lips and throat still burning, we walk through the night market which takes over Zhongshanlu between 7.30pm and 2am every night. The crowds are out and a large group has gathered in front of a counter set up on a street corner, where a charismatic guy with a microphone is auctioning off electronic items, such as shavers and hairdryers. People seem to be getting bargains for as little as 2 Yuan but nothing goes unsold and the auction is conducted at a breakneck pace. They obviously have a lot of stuff to get through.

We stand hypnotised by the frenetic activity but eventually manage to tear ourselves away and walk into a nearby park to watch a mid-river fountain display. All the trees and bridges along the Li and its tributaries are brightly lit and colourfully decorated at night and the park is full of folk enjoying the warm evening.

The next morning we are up early as our plan is to rent bicycles and ride off into the countryside. Sofie and I have vastly different cycling histories and are at opposite ends of the cycling ability spectrum. I haven't ridden a bike for forty years while she, being Belgian, has cycling in her blood. She is a complete natural and sets off at a pace I cannot hope to match, sailing confidently over intersections and navigating her way easily through the crazy Guilin traffic. All I can do is follow in her wake and gaze admiringly at her back as it disappears into the distant haze.

We have decided to head for a place called Reed Flute Cave, about five kilometres out of town. The ride out there is pretty easy once you get beyond the chaos of the town centre and we quickly find ourselves in a rural sprawl of small villages and paddy fields, punctuated by almost vertical limestone pinnacles covered in bright green vegetation.

We lock the bicycles together next to a small police post and climb up to the entrance. The Reed Flute Cave is an underground system of staggering beauty, decorated with stalactites that hang from the ceiling like elaborate ivory carvings and stalagmites over forty metres tall. The centrepiece is a massive hall named the Crystal Palace, which is said to be able to hold 6,000 people and famously provided shelter for the citizens of Guilin during Japanese air raids in the 1937 – 1945 war. We spend almost an hour walking around following a guide who shows us a series of glorious light shows highlighting features of the cave system. Fortunately, she resists the temptation to break into song.

In the evening, we head into town again, looking for dinner options. Without thinking, we fall victim to the Lonely Planet effect and end up in the same Szechuan place as last night. The huge LP logo is on a signboard on the street above the entrance, advertising the fact that it is mentioned in the Guide, and 75% of the clientele is Caucasian. We reflect on why we have elected to return to this restaurant when there are so many alternatives and conclude that it is because the prices are reasonable, the food is great, the service is friendly and in a town full of touts and with a bad reputation for ripping travellers off, it is a safe choice. It is a question of trust and, throughout our long trip, Lonely Planet has proven trustworthy.

After dinner we walk over the river to Elephant Hill Park, turn a corner and find ourselves confronted by an astonishing sight. Over a hundred people are ballroom dancing in the open air, swirling in harmony between the low walls of a small, darkened courtyard while music emanates from a CD player hidden away in the shadows. Some distance further on, next to an avenue of flowerbeds, four rows of ladies are line dancing in perfect unison. We watch them entranced - it must be something in the air.

And that is it: the final wonderful experience on a wonderful journey. The next morning we leave terra firma for the first time in two months and fly. We are bound for Bali, where we plan to live, via stops in Kuala Lumpur, Malaysia to see old friends and then Singapore to pick up visas. We have loved travelling overland, under the flight path. We have been fascinated by these huge, complex, intriguing countries, which, for so long, I thought I would never be able to visit.

We give silent thanks to all the people in Russia, Mongolia and China we have met along the way, who have delighted us with their hospitality, enhanced our experience and shared their wisdom with us. We recognise that any knowledge and understanding we have acquired from our brief contact is just superficial. We want to return to spend more time and learn more. When? As soon as possible. Before we have left, we start planning a return journey, perhaps via the Silk Road and the 'Stans: politics, wars and other obstacles permitting.

Oh yes, and we have not missed flying at all: the endless processing queues, the feeling of being imprisoned in a narrow aluminium tube at 30,000 feet and having to be seated for hours on end. And we have definitely not missed the jetlag.

Home at Last

"Welcome home!"

Made's smiling face, wreathed in good nature, beams at us over the greeting fence as we emerge from Customs into the heat of Bali at midday. As he has just been to the temple, he is wearing a white head-dress, has a flower tucked behind his ear and a couple of grains of rice stuck to his forehead.

A folded, green, banana-leaf offering tray containing flower petals, candy and an un-smoked cigarette is perched under the windscreen of his van. Made explains that the van has just been blessed too.

It is already apparent that we are entering a strange new world and we haven't even left the airport car park yet.

But that is another story.

Appendices

Notes from short stops en route to Moscow

The story I tell in Under the Flight Path begins in Moscow, but our overland journey did not start there. First we had to get to Moscow and the following notes were scribbled during our journey from Sofie's hometown of Ghent, via Köln in Germany, Warsaw in Poland, Vilnius in Lithuania and Riga in Latvia.   I thought readers might be interested in seeing these too.

Köln, Germany

If you are travelling across Europe by train, Köln is a great place to break your journey for a few hours. There are automatic left luggage machines in the concourse so you don't have to lug your bags around town, there is a little supermarket in the station to stock up on supplies and, best of all, the magnificent Gothic pile of Köln Cathedral sits right outside the station. The cathedral is stunning: immense and imposing on the outside, light and airy inside. It is incredible that it survived the World War 2 bombing campaigns that completely levelled the city around it.

In front of the entrance to the cathedral, there is a full-size model of one of the sculptures that top out the towers. It is staggering to compare its bulk with the real one all the way up there, which looks so tiny from the ground.

Right by the cathedral are the main City Museum and the Modern Art Gallery and it is only a short walk to the Rhine and the Old Town with its outdoor cafes and cobbled squares. On a sunny Sunday afternoon in April, hippies and punks rub shoulders comfortably and non-threateningly with monks and nuns, each taking refuge in the company of their own kind, and the grassy park and promenade next to the river are alive with entwined couples and strolling families. If you feel the need, there are a couple of Irish bars in the Old Town, havens of English-speaking where you can catch up with the latest Premier League football.

Warsaw, Poland

Warsaw is pretty much a brand new city. We were advised that the place to go in order to understand why this is so, is the Uprising Museum at ul. Grzybowska 79. The excellent "In Your Pocket" guide calls it the best museum in Poland.

There is plenty of information about the exhibits in English and, after spending an hour touring the three floors of highly creative, interactive exhibits, we a) are astonished that Warsaw even exists today and b) marvel at the immense courage and resilience of the Polish people.

If you visit the Uprising Museum at the beginning of a trip to Warsaw, it will put everything else you see in the city into perspective.

Between 1939 and 1945 Warsaw and its population were systematically annihilated by occupying German forces until there was virtually nothing left. The city owes its existence today to a massive sixty-year rebuilding programme begun by the communist government that ran Poland as a client state of the Soviet Union until the Berlin Wall came down.

The programme continues to this day. Even in April 2009, in the midst of a worldwide financial meltdown, tall cranes still punctuate the skyline and exotically sculpted towers of glass and steel compete for our admiration.

But the tallest building is still the cheap knock-off copy of the Empire State Building that towers over the central railway station, a gift from the Peoples of the Soviet Union, built in three years and an eighth sibling for Stalin's seven sisters in Moscow. We will later see a ninth sibling in Riga. It is called the palace of Culture and Science and there is a viewing platform thirty floors up, which offers bird's eye views of the city.

The old town is clean, bright, spacious and perfectly laid out. This is, of course, because it is not old at all, it is just built that way, reconstructed post-war with bricks recovered from the rubble and millions more donated by towns in the German west of Poland who demolished their own historic buildings, for example the magnificent Szczecin Opera House, to facilitate the rebirth of their capital.

A wonderful place to walk around on a sunny day is Lazienki Park, Warsaw's green lung situated to the south of the city, close to the antenna-festooned mansions of Embassy Row. Red squirrels hop easily from branch to branch but the peacocks look far less comfortable in the trees. A few are perching awkwardly and noisily on high branches and seem to be constantly on the verge of crashing to the ground. They are much more elegant and in their element when they are strolling around with their feet safely on the ground. It is an idyllic place to relax away from the bustle of the city. The Chopin memorial is here in the middle of a rose garden, just next to the Belvedere Palace on ul. Belvederska.

In the evening we don't bother with the flash glitzy nightspots but head instead for a student club offering live music. The feature act on the night is Perfect, Poland's top 1970s hair-rock band. The line up still includes the original lead singer and songwriter, a national icon and part of the fabric of Polish pop culture. He needs a bit of a sit-down every few songs nowadays but remembers all the words and inspires fervour among a thousand-strong audience. He still has the energy to do not just one encore but two!

Warsaw is a modern city with an important history that should be part of every man's universal education. The violence that the city and its people were subjected to, the heroism with which they responded, the way their suffering was ignored by an uncaring world that turned its gaze away and the attempts by the post-war Polish governments to conceal and manipulate what happened all make for an essential 20th century story. This was a extraordinarily shameful episode in the most shameful of centuries. The story is hard to hear as it implicates those who would seek to derive glory and vindication from "victory" in the Second World War but it is a story that should be heard by all.

Vilnius, Lithuania

We arrive in Vilnius on the train from Warsaw via Sestokai. It is the 2009 European City of Culture and a beautiful little place with a wonderful, quaint old town, best seen on a sunny spring day with blue skies and a light breeze coming off the river.

Everywhere is walk-able and strolling between the main sights takes you through cobbled streets and past buildings decorated in a variety of eclectic ways. Many are painted in vibrant colours. There are white mini-palaces, pink churches, townhouses in pastel shades of blue and green. It all results in a chaotic blend of styles that somehow fit perfectly.

Recent occupying neighbours may have tried to destroy the culture of Vilnius and Lithuania as a whole, but one small comfort is that they did not destroy the architecture here, as they did in Warsaw.

The attempted destruction of Lithuanian culture and the wholesale murder, deportation and enslavement of its people is told in all its gory detail in the unique, sobering and powerful exhibits contained in the Genocide Museum. It occupies the building in central Vilnius that was formerly occupied by the KGB until their forced, hurried departure in 1991. Much of the furniture has been left exactly as it was when they vacated the premises and there are still bags of shredded documents piled against one of the office walls.

It is a grim place and makes for difficult viewing at times but it does help the visitor understand what the people of this country had to endure during five decades of occupation and how much they have done to repair the damage of that era in the eighteen years since independence. The most affecting section of the museum is the prison on the ground floor, left exactly as it was with padded cells, exercise courtyards and an execution chamber which, even on a warm day, leaves you shivering.

Every person who walks the streets of Vilnius today bears the scars of the Soviet occupation. It is so recent. The faces that look down from the photographs on the walls of the Genocide Museum today, both torturers and victims, are the fathers and grandfathers of today's shop assistants, waiters, bus drivers, workers, managers, rich and poor. Those who helped the Russians and those who fought them, either with silent resentment or shouting out loud, all walk the streets of free, independent Vilnius today. Everybody looks the same to us, but they all know who is who.

An additional legacy of the Soviet era is the silence of the crowds in the town centre of Vilnius even now, that echoes a time when a casual public remark made within the hearing of a KGB informant, (there were 6,000 on the books in Vilnius alone,) could lead to the dreaded midnight knock on the door. We will notice a similar phenomenon later in this trip, in the Moscow metro.

Riga, Latvia

For most of us in English-speaking countries, the Second World War is remote and resides only in Poppy Day, grandfathers' memories and movies like Saving Private Ryan. Just as for Lithuanians, for Latvians the Second World War did not end in 1945. It ended in 1991, when independence from the Soviet Union finally put an end to the foreign occupation of their country.

The secret Molotov-Ribbentrop non-aggression pact of 1939 gave the Soviet Union rights to Latvia and the Red Army marched in a year later to begin a fifty-year period of oppression that was interrupted only by a three-year period of oppression by Nazi Germany between 1941 and 1944. The Soviet Union's first short period of tenure culminated in the deportation to Siberia of tens of thousands of Latvians aboard cattle wagons and when the Nazis arrived a month later they were initially greeted as liberators.

The ensuing massacre of Riga's Jewish population and other groups, then the forced application of Latvia's industry to the German war effort, swiftly showed that the Nazis were no liberators. When the Red Army returned in 1944, to finish what they had started, this time Latvians had no illusions and hundreds of thousands fled. Those that were left were rounded up, categorised and organised. 42,000 people were dispatched to Siberian labour camps in 1949 alone.

Only after the 1956 "thaw" that followed Khrushchev's denunciation of Stalin's purges and mass deportations, did they gradually begin to return. However, they were now much, much fewer in number. Thousands had already died in the camps or en route to the camps and many found it impossible to return to Soviet Latvia because they were branded as undesirable elements. The whole period of Soviet and Nazi control, the efforts of both regimes to subjugate the Latvian people and destroy their culture, and the developments that eventually led to independence after fifty years, are recorded in painful detail in the Museum of the Occupation of Latvia, an essential part of any visit to Riga. It is in the Old Town, next to St Peter's Church and right on the river. Most of the exhibits are described in English and entry is free of charge.

We are sickened and stunned by the evidence presented in exhibit after exhibit of the depth and extent of the systematic programme of attrition carried out against the Baltic peoples. During our stay in Riga, we are fortunate to have the chance to speak to local people who were personally affected by these events and for whom the emotional scars have yet to heal. It is unlikely that they ever will.

We speak to Janis, an 85-year-old man who was conscripted into the Latvian legion of the German Army as a teenager and fought against the Red Army as it pushed the Germans back across Eastern and Central Europe. The Latvian legion fought bravely, its soldiers earning twelve Iron Crosses and, through dogged rear-guard action as the Soviet forces advanced on Latvia in 1944, the Legion created an opportunity for 200,000 Latvian citizens to escape to Sweden, the USA and elsewhere before the Red Army arrived.

These efforts earned Janis and his brothers-in-arms two years in an internment camp in Belarus where over 60% of the inmates died of starvation. When Janis starts to speak of this time his eyes glaze over and he stops abruptly, unwilling to dig further into memories of things that we probably would not understand anyway. From Belarus, those who survived were brought back to Riga and interned there until they were selected by factory bosses and returned to society with jobs and a place to live.

But Janis' sentence was not over, For the next three decades Janis and his wife were subjected to taunts of "Nazi" and "Fascist" everywhere they went from neighbours loyal to the new Soviet-sponsored regime. Janis and his wife were prohibited from using the special stores, access to which was restricted only to the communist party elite. They remember that the members of the elite could always eat well even when there was nothing in the usual shops. For fifty years they had to watch what they said, watch what they did and always be aware that someone, somewhere was watching them. Even smiling in the street could get them arrested. Simply speaking Latvian instead of Russian was to invite criticism.

Even now after independence, when Janis and his former comrades meet to honour the fallen dead of World War 2, they face protests and are labelled as neo-Nazis by the media. Janis is evidently still upset at the unfairness of this. He emphasises with some force that he and his comrades had little choice. They were conscripted by one invader and fought FOR their country against a second invader.

We also speak to Aivars, born in a labour camp in Omsk, Siberia in 1951 to a twenty-year old Latvian girl, who had been deported two years earlier simply because she owned two homes, a consequence of the rest of her family having fled to Sweden in

1944. They returned to Latvia in 1956 but throughout his life, until independence in 1991, Aivars, an exceptionally gifted student, was denied opportunities to travel and other benefits because of his "bad biography".

Janis is Sofie's great uncle on her mother's side. Alvars is a friend of the family. Sofie's great-grandmother was a nurse who, in 1944, escaped from Latvia with her parents, brother and son (Sofie's grandfather) ahead of the return of the Red Army. Her husband remained in Latvia. She eventually arrived in France after the armistice, crossing the Elbe into allied hands after working in a German concentration camp, where she met, cared for and eventually escaped with her future husband, a French prisoner.

Sofie asks Janis about her great-grandfather, whose name was Zhanis. Neither she nor any of the family now living in Belgium has ever heard the story of what happened to him. They only know that he died before the end of the Soviet occupation.

Janis tells Sofie that Zhanis was incarcerated by the KGB in Riga from 1944 to 1946, along with 53 other members of a Latvian Independence movement, including Latvia's then President. At their trial in 1946, three of the members of the movement were sentenced to death. Zhanis, along with the others, was sentenced to ten years in a labour camp in Novosibirsk, Siberia.

An additional penalty of five years was later imposed but following the 1956 general amnesty, Zhanis was released. He returned to Latvia that year. It took him a month to get home, riding on top of trains and eating grain from the cracks in the floor of cattle wagons. He was fifty years old. Somehow his time in the labour camps had made him stone deaf, so, on his return, he could not work and was put on a state pension. He died in a house fire in 1983. Everyone else in the building escaped. He may have been asleep and, with his lack of hearing, the noise of the fire and people shouting failed to wake him.

Janis's revelations fill a huge and important gap in Sofie's family history and clarify things that have remained unexplained for over sixty years. When Latvia disappeared behind the iron curtain, communication with the West was almost impossible. Sofie's grandfather returned to his homeland after independence to try to find his father, but was too late. If he learned about Zhanis's experience in the Gulag, he never mentioned it when he went back to Belgium.

Quite apart from learning about the important recent history of this country, which, on its own, makes Riga worth visiting, it is a beautiful place to spend a few days. We arrive on the last weekend in April, the first weekend of summer, and the colours of the buildings in the Old Town and the Art Nouveau district glow in the sunshine. The cafes open out onto the squares in the late afternoon, the girls are in their summer dresses and the northern sky is an unbroken blue. The economic crisis has bitten hard in Latvia but the city still bustles gently and the taste of construction and renovation lies in the air.

A unique and rewarding experience is offered by the 100-plus hectares of the Latvian Ethnographic Museum on the edge of Riga. It was founded in 1924 and its existence bears witness to an extraordinary vision of the need to preserve rural Latvian ways for future generations. That it survived the cultural annihilation of the Soviet era is even more astonishing. Perhaps, as it was lost and overgrown in the forest, it escaped notice. But post-1991 it has been restored, developed and lovingly nurtured to become a living, breathing tribute to the past.

Wooden buildings dating back to the early sixteenth century, including churches, farmhouses, granaries, windmills and a country inn, have been transported to the site and rebuilt in village environments typical of the region of Latvia where they were originally found. The whole park is an idyllic spot, in the middle of a pine forest on the edge of a large lake. You can sample a variety of basic Latvian dishes from the various food outlets and walk around houses furnished exactly as they were when they were occupied and in daily use. Indeed, the two 500-year-old wooden churches on the site are still working buildings and we are lucky enough to come upon one while a Sunday morning service is being held. We spend a few minutes watching the congregation receiving communion below a decorated sky-blue ceiling and to the sound of an ancient organ playing at the back of the hall.

With one more day in Riga and a car at our disposal, we head out of town to Sigulda, where urban Latvians go to play. There are castles, long sandy beaches, skiing in winter and you can even try out an Olympic size bobsleigh run if you are feeling brave. The coastline is glorious, the Baltic Sea is as flat and clear as glass, albeit bitterly cold to paddle in, and a bit of sharp-eyed beach-combing by Sofie actually turns up a piece of amber.

Tomorrow, we take the train into Russia. It will be two months before we see the ocean again.

Crossing the Border

A short story written for a competition, based on our experience crossing the border into Mongolia

The officer is sitting marooned on an island of furniture in the centre of the room, which has bright green walls and smells of fresh paint. I stand almost at attention in front of him. A single bare light-bulb hangs above us and shadows deepen the dark semi-circles beneath his eyes as he leans forward to write, my passport open on the desk in front of him. I know that my expression must reflect my anxiety so I avert my gaze: a notice board on the wall carries one item, a faded FBI Most Wanted poster for Osama Bin Laden. The officer grunts to get my attention and I tense in anticipation but he doesn't look up. Instead, with one wave of an expressive hand he manages both to let me know that the interview is over and to instruct the soldier at the door to escort me back to the train.

The coaches sit engine-less at the cold dark platform. My first class compartment should be a warm, cosy refuge but I am far from comfortable and examine the floor nervously to see if anything has been disturbed.

This is frontier control at Sukhbaatar, an outpost in the southern Gobi half a world away from St Pancras where my journey began three months ago and a place where, just a few minutes ago, I was convinced my journey was going to come to an abrupt, premature end. I am still not sure if I am safe.

All is quiet on the train now and the platform is dim and deserted except for two bored soldiers lounging against a lamppost. It was not like that half an hour ago when we pulled in to see a mass of armed police welcoming us to Mongolia amidst a bizarre production of flashing lights and martial music.

Normally, I would have found this entertaining but I was still in shock after what had just taken place in the darkness between the border fences. Shortly after leaving the Russian control point at Naushki the train had shuddered to a halt. There was activity outside in the corridor and suddenly my compartment door was thrown open by a grim-faced lady train-guard. In the corridor behind her were a group of people; all carrying bulging red, blue and white striped zippered carrier bags.

She said something brusque to me in Russian then bent and pulled the central strip of carpet back to expose a hatch. She opened it with a flick of her wrist and stood aside to allow one of the men clustered at the door to come in. I watched bewildered from my bunk as he and the others formed a human chain to transfer one carrier bag after another into the hatch. The hole seemed to extend far beyond the walls of the compartment and it must have taken them ten minutes to stow everything away. The guard closed the hatch and replaced the carpet carefully, glancing at me on her way out with a half smile, which may have been intended to reassure but which singularly failed in its aim.

When I saw the welcoming party on the platform at Sukhbaatar, my heart sank and my feeling of impending doom increased when the music stopped and I heard a riot of shouting and banging as the police made their way through the train checking papers, ferreting through bags, peering under seats and tapping wall panels.

The first uniform through my door held out his hand and said "passport." He flicked through it, frowned and beckoned me. "Come," he said and walked me off the train and into the green, newly painted office in the station building. I waited with dread while he made his report, wondering what was going on in my compartment while I stood there. "Wrong visa," said the seated officer, "fifty dollars!" I handed over the cash without argument and watched him begin his paperwork before being dismissed.

Back on the train, I sit in ignorance and trepidation. Did they look beneath the carpet? Did they open the hatch? What did they find? Do they think I am involved? Are they coming back? The platform lights flash on and a squad of policemen approach. My passport, with a brand new visa inside, is returned. The police leave, the train jolts as our new engine is attached and with a blast of the horn we are on our way again. The sound of wild cheering echoes down the corridor and the guard appears once again in my doorway, smiling broadly this time as she supervises the removal of the undetected contraband. I cannot help but smile back. The world is at my feet once more: for a moment there I thought it was all going to be taken away.

An Ice Diving Safari in Russia's Galapagos

An article written for a scuba diving magazine.

Siberia's Lake Baikal is a magical destination, a place of superlatives and amazing statistics. It is the oldest, deepest lake on the planet and contains 20% of the world's unfrozen fresh water. It occupies an area the size of France, is fed by 330 rivers and drained by only one, the Angara. Often called "Russia's Galapagos", Baikal's age and isolation have combined to produce incredible biodiversity. It is home to over 1,700 species of plants and animals, two-thirds of which are found nowhere else.

The changing seasons offer vastly different experiences for visitors but the most challenging and rewarding time to go there is late winter/early spring when the lake delivers beautiful scenery, myriad opportunities for winter sports and the most unique ice-diving experience anywhere. In February and March, the ice is so thick that you can drive across it and interlocking sheets of ice create a spectacular landscape of ridges and canyons.

You fly into Irkutsk at the southwest end of the lake or you can take the more leisurely option: fly to Moscow or Beijing and catch a Trans-Siberian train, four days in each direction. Our recommendation? Take a buddy and go first class in a private two-person compartment, as we did.

From Irkutsk you join a convoy of 4-wheel drive vehicles and head up to Olkhon Island in mid-lake where the village of Khuzir acts as base camp for the safari. The truly adventurous can continue further north where the wild Ushkany archipelago is home to a large colony of unique fresh water seals called "nerpa", fat, furry little guys with big eyes and funny faces.

The usual programme covers seven days and involves one ice dive a day. You will also have plenty of opportunity to explore the world above the ice, photograph the gorgeous, other-worldly natural ice sculptures, walk on completely clear fields of frozen water or explore ice caves formed by freezing surf.

In the evening you can enjoy the mobile sauna and be introduced to the delights of "Banya", an essential life-enhancing Siberian experience featuring super hot steam baths followed by quick dips in the icy waters of the lake and beatings with freshly cut leafy twigs. Of course, the last two elements are entirely optional but what a story you will have to tell.

When you scuba dive under the ice, you can look up to a fabulous, intricately decorated white glass ceiling and down to a dramatic, bright green world decorated with huge tree-like sponges. Small fish flit among the undergrowth and incredible alien-looking crustaceans known as amphipods are everywhere. There are over 250 species of them, all unique to Baikal.

If you have not ice-dived before, use the first two or three days to take a course. Yes, this is extreme diving but the challenge is mental rather than physical. Diving in an overhead environment is not for the claustrophobic and you should have good skills and the ability to remain calm underwater.

Take a drysuit if you have one or you can always rent one there. Don't even think about diving in a wetsuit. You will use single cylinders equipped with a dual outlet valve, so in addition to your normal dive gear you will need to take a separate regulator first stage for your octopus. Each of your two regulators should have its own contents gauge too and it is good practice to have your BCD inflator attached to one regulator and your drysuit inflator to the other.

When the ice is on the lake, the skies are usually clear and, while the temperature can rise above zero during the day, at night it will plummet to as low as minus 20C. So pack a quilted jacket with a hood, a strong pair of boots or shoes, thermal underwear, thick woollen socks, a woolly hat and gloves. Don't forget a pair of sunglasses too, to protect your eyes from the glare.

The combination of mystical Baikal, the frozen lake-scapes and diving under the ice of the deepest lake on earth combine to make this one of the most fulfilling and rewarding dive travel experiences you could ever wish for.

Taking the Train in China Today

The rail network in China has undergone a phenomenal transformation in the years since we made the journey retold in Under the Flight Path. Today, super-fast, super-slick bullet trains have transformed travel on major inter-city routes. Having said that, travel by train on minor routes is still exactly the same as we experienced it.

The clever folk at China DIY Travel have put together some excellent advice for foreigners travelling by train in China today and I have reproduced this in the following paragraphs. We have booked tickets by email with China DIY Travel on several occasions and have found this advice very useful.

Most bullet trains (G trains) depart from modern train stations that were recently built to handle this type of train. The new stations are mostly located out of town and food outlets are minimal. Other categories of train depart from older stations, which are often in very well developed parts of town with tons of restaurants. While newer stations have escalators, older stations may only have stairs to get to the platform. Note that stairs generally have a ramp on both sides. These are for rolling suitcases.

In many cities, there is more than one train station. So make sure that you know which one your train is departing from. You may arrive in a city at one station and depart from another.

In the older stations there may be minimal signage in English. The smaller the town, the less English signage you will find. Public announcements are generally made only in Mandarin except in larger cities. You are unlikely to find many staff that speak English.

The station entrance is generally located in the middle of the building. However, you need to have a ticket before you enter the station. Ticket offices are located either to the left or to the right of the entrance. Or there may be two, one on each side. In some rare cases, the ticket office may be on a lower floor. The office is usually well indicated in English. In very small towns, you may have to walk around a bit to find it. In some places you may have to pass your luggage through an x-ray machine just to enter the ticket office.

You may see signs for "electronic tickets"," automatic tickets" "automatic fetching" or similar terms. These are automatic distributors only for Chinese citizens, who can get tickets using their national ID card.

You can pick up any train ticket at any train station in China. If you bought tickets online for several trains, you can pick up all your tickets at one train station although there will be a five Yuan service fee per ticket if your train departs from another city. That is, if you are at the Xian train station and you want to pick up paper tickets for Shanghai to Beijing, the ticket office at the train station in Xian will charge you a service fee of 5 Yuan per ticket.

If you are running out of time to pick up tickets purchased online, you can always cut in the front of the line. Use body language such as pointing to your watch, and, most importantly, smile! Chinese people are usually friendly. They will let you cut in. One person can pick-up all the tickets for a group but will need to present a passport for each person.

If you have problems finding the ticket office, look for Chinese people who look like students. They will be wearing glasses and will be carrying their own luggage. Some students can understand English although their spoken English may not be very good. If the first person you stop cannot help, try another.

Carry your passport. You will need it to buy or pick up tickets and your passport will be compared with the name on your ticket before you are allowed access to the station and waiting rooms.

In the ticket office, join any of the queues. You may find that one or two queues look suspiciously short. These are probably the lines for ticket exchange or refunds. As you can't read the Chinese sign above the counter, you can't really tell. So try these counters in any case. You might be lucky. Sometimes, acting like a stupid tourist pays off. If not, all they will do is wave you off to one of the other counters.

Once you have your tickets, go back outside and enter the station via the central entrance. Present your passport and ticket then pass a very basic x-ray security check to get into the departure area.

Once you are there, look for your waiting hall and departure gate on one of the screens. If you are not sure which is the waiting hall / departure gate for your train, just show your ticket to someone who looks like they work there and they will point you in the right direction.

You may see signs indicating waiting rooms for travellers holding tickets for soft seats, soft sleepers or VIP tickets. Ignore these rooms. They can be traps. You can't see the signs in the main waiting area and the announcements are not as easy to hear. These special waiting rooms just make it easier for you to miss your train.

Passengers are let onto the platform train by train. The train currently boarding is indicated on a sign next to or above the ticket barrier. When your train number changes colour on the electronic signboard at the barrier gate, this tells you that you can board the train. This will normally happen 10 to 15 minutes before the scheduled departure time. The colour change is usually yellow to green but we have also seen green to yellow. When the train number goes red that means boarding is closed. This usually happens five minutes before the train will leave.

Sometimes you access the platform by inserting your ticket into an electronic reader. Or a railway employee will be waiting to check your ticket, scan it or punch a hole in it to validate it. Sometimes, on very busy trains, you just walk through the barrier. Do what everybody else does.

Don't panic. There is no need to rush. If you are in the crowd heading for the train, you will make it. The trains load very fast. We have seen several hundred people board a train in under five minutes. Nobody is left on the platform.

But you do need to be prepared for the boarding announcement. This is not the time to be caught repacking bags or half way through eating a sandwich. Again, follow the other passengers. Do what they do.

Your carriage and seat number are shown on the top right of your ticket. The carriage number comes first, then the seat number. Carriage numbers are shown prominently on the carriage. Some trains are very long. If you are waiting on the platform and don't know where your carriage will pull up when the train arrives, show your ticket to an employee on the platform. They will point you in the right direction. In many stations there are actually markings on the floor, showing where each carriage will stop, and waiting passengers form an orderly queue behind these, (really!)

The carriage attendant will sometimes check your ticket before you board the train and the conductor will pass through the train to check it again once you are moving.

If you are travelling by sleeper train, wear comfortable clothes, buy a bottle of water ahead of time and, if you have ear plugs, bring them. Take your own toilet paper. Don't pack your toothbrush too deep in your luggage, as you will want to freshen up in the morning.

When you board a sleeper train, the conductor will exchange your ticket for a plastic token with your sleeper number on it. Before the train arrives at the station where you will disembark, the conductor will return and give you your ticket back. This tells you that your stop is approaching. So, if you are disembarking from the train in the middle of the night, the conductor will be your wake up call. Nevertheless, it is a good idea to set your alarm too, just in case.

On all trains, if you are getting off at an intermediate station, make sure you know your time of arrival, as the announcement for the next station may be in Mandarin only. On newer trains there is an overhead electronic signboard in Chinese and English that gives you next stop information, train speed, current time and inside / outside temperature. On older trains, sometimes the conductor just sticks his head into the car and yells the name of the next stop. Always make sure that it is really your stop. If in doubt, show your ticket to fellow travellers. As the train is about to stop, look out of the window to check the station name on the pillars or signboards.

Be aware that sometimes the train turns around. Well it doesn't actually turn around, but sometimes it needs to go back the way it came. Therefore, all the seats need to turn around, so passengers will still be facing in the same direction that the train is going. All rows of seats on the newer Chinese trains are reversible. They swivel on a central point and movement is activated by pressing on a foot pedal. As a foreigner, you won't be expected to do anything other than pick up your stuff and get out of the way. One of your fellow passengers will take care of the engineering.

When you exit from your arrival station, you will often need to show your ticket or pass it through an electronic gate. So don't leave it on the train and keep it handy.

Acknowledgements

My name may be on the cover of this book but it belongs just as much to my wife Sofie, who shared these adventures and edited, proof-read and approved the final version.

A huge Spaseeba goes to our great friend, journalist and diver extraordinaire Andrey Bizyukin, who introduced us to many of the folk who helped make our Russian odyssey so entertaining and interesting. Thanks to Oleg, Svetlana, Gleb and Anna for the trip into the Altai and especially to Gleb for the dive in Teletskoye. Gennady Misan knows Lake Baikal underwater better than anyone in the world and I am grateful to him for lending us the equipment and allowing us to join him and his students in the cold, green water. In Irkutsk, it was great to meet the three Annas and hear their stories.

Tsetsegee enabled us to travel through Mongolia outside the usual season and chose the perfect travelling companions: Adya because of his expertise, the other two for the entertainment.

Thanks are also due to Tomek and Ania Stopyra for guiding us in Warsaw, Maris and Martins Baldonieks for organising our Riga visit and Sergei Volnuhin and Vladimir Timofeev for their wonderful hospitality during our stay in Moscow. I am grateful too to my good friend Tim Rock and my cousin, the talented author Jackie Winter, for their advice on the final draft.

And finally, as always, I must mention the folk at Createspace, Kindle and Audible, the publishing outlets without whom none of this would be possible.

Bibliography

Before and during the trip we read the following books. These both enhanced our journey and helped us make the right choices.

The Terracotta Army by John Man, Bantam, 2008

In Siberia by Colin Thubron, Harper Collins, 2000

Lonely Planet Trans-Siberian (Travel Guide)

Lonely Planet China (Travel Guide)

Finally, our advice would be never to embark on any train travel anywhere in the world without first seeking the advice of 'The Man in Seat Sixty-One.' (**www.seat61.com**)

About the Author

Simon Pridmore is the author of a number of scuba diving and travel guides. He formerly worked as a civil servant in Hong Kong before becoming a professional diver and itinerant writer. He and his wife Sofie live and plot further adventures in Bali, Indonesia.

Also by Simon Pridmore

Scuba Confidential - An Insider's Guide to Becoming a Better Diver (Sandsmedia, Indonesia, 2013)

Scuba Professional – Insights into Sport Diver Training & Operations (Sandsmedia, Indonesia, 2015)

Scuba Fundamental – Start Diving the Right Way (Sandsmedia, Indonesia, 2016)

Diving & Snorkeling Guide to Bali (with Tim Rock) (Doubleblue / Mantaray Publishing, USA 2013: Second Edition 2016)

Diving & Snorkeling Guide to Raja Ampat and Northeast Indonesia (with Tim Rock) (Doubleblue / Mantaray Publishing, USA 2016)

Made in the USA
San Bernardino, CA
18 December 2017